FAITH IT—'TIL YOU MAKE IT!

Ben Tankard

www.Faith-It-Til-You-Make-It.com

Faith It—'til You Make It!

"Now faith is the substance of things hoped for,
the evidence of things not seen."
Hebrews 11: 1

by Ben Tankard

Ben-Jamin' Publishing
(A Division of Ben Tankard Ministries)
Murfreesboro, TN 37129
Unless otherwise indicated, all Scripture quotations are
taken from the *King James Version* of the Bible.

Faith It—'til You Make It
ISBN 0-9718580-0-4
Printed in the United States of America
Copyright ©2002 by Ben Tankard
P.O. Box 11594
Murfreesboro, TN 37129
(615) 207-6685 phone
(615) 907-6729 fax
www.bentankardministries.com
bentankard@aol.com

Published by:
Ben-Jamin' Publishing (A Division of Ben Tankard
Ministries)
P.O. Box 11594
Murfreesboro, TN 37129

Printed in the United States of America

What Others Are Saying About…

Ben Tankard and *Faith It—'til You Make It!*

"Ben Tankard has struck a chord the body of Christ needs to hear as he speaks to us about the significant role faith plays in helping us attain our God-given goals without compromising the deeper treasure of inner harmony with God."

Bishop T.D. Jakes / The Potter's House, Inc.

"My friend Ben Tankard and I came out of college the same year with the same goals—professional basketball. I went on to a successful career in the NBA, but Ben's dreams were dashed by a side-lining injury. However, through his walk of faith he has become equally as successful in his career as a top recording artist and faith teacher. His story is motivating and his message is anointed. He has been a true inspiration to me for many years and I am honored to say that we are partnering on several projects together. If you want to win in life this book is for you!

Wayman Tisdale / Phoenix Suns

"Ben Tankard, a gifted and talented recording artist, who has dedicated his gifts to the Lord!"

Dr. Frederick K.C. Price / Crenshaw Christian Center

"I have enjoyed Ben's music and ministry over the last decade. This book has my endorsement!"

A.C. Green / Dallas Mavericks / A.C. Green Foundation

"Ben Tankard is one of the most anointed young men in ministry today. I am so blessed by how he has allowed God to use his many gifts to change lives all over the world. He is a marvelous example of what the power of God can do when a man makes a decision to yield to the will of the Father for his life. Taffi and I could not be more proud of what he has accomplished. Keep up the good work, Ben!"

Dr. Creflo Dollar / World Changers Ministries International

"The Most powerful force on earth is faith, because it is the substance of hope. When a person loses hope, he loses the reason to live. Faith is the only substance that pleases God and the "Just" must live by it. In this work, *Faith It— 'til You Make It!*, Ben Tankard gives us an inspirational injection for our personal faith, and motivates us by his faith to use ours in the adventure of life. Everyone should read this book and hear this message. Great work!"

Dr. Myles Munroe / Bahamas Faith Ministries International

"Ben Tankard is a true champion! *Faith It— 'til You Make It!*, will challenge you to go to a new level in your faith walk with God. Ben's testimony is something we can all gain inspiration from. By God's power, as a top music artist, speaker and now a writer, he is using his talents to influence the world for righteousness. Great job, Ben!"

Darrell Green / Washington Redskins - Darrell Green Youth Life Foundation

Tankard has become one of the top producers in Gospel. The blessings keep on coming. This is just the beginning!

USA Today

Dedication / Acknowledgements

A special thanks to these people who, in some way, contributed to the completion and success of this, my first book.

— — —

To God, thank You for Your awesome presence in my life, and for the gift to minister Your Word to Your people through music, teaching, impartation and example.

To my late parents, Arthur and Mary Tankard, for bringing me into this world and for hearing from God and naming me "Benjamin," a derivative of the great man who was the son of Jacob.

To my lovely wife Jewel, for her undying support, and to our children, Marcus, 17, Brooklyn, 13, Britney, 11, Benji, 10, and Cyrene, 6, for sharing Daddy with the rest of the world. I love you all. You're the best!

To my anointed, and loving sisters, Patrice and Avaleir. Thank you for sharing your lives and love with me. It was a blessing growing up with you.

To my editor, Ron Jordan, for your patience over the past three years through my endless changes and additions. You have done a great job of capturing my heart.

To Russ Harrington for the great photography and Tim Parker for the brilliant graphic design.

To my good friends Rick Hayes and Vic Bolten (World Changers), Larry Carpenter (FaithWorks Distributing), and Daniel Lavan (Rhema Publishing), for teamwork and unselfish contributions in making the "Ben-Jamin' Publishing" dream a reality.

I also give special honor to my spiritual bloodline, which includes the Jacob in my life, Dr. Rick Layton, my spiritual father; the Isaac in my life, Dr. Creflo A. Dollar Jr., my spiritual grandfather; and the Abraham (father of Faith) in my life, Evangelist Kenneth Copeland, my spiritual great grandfather. It takes a village to raise a child and you all truly "raised" me in the spirit.

I also honor Dr. Fredrick K.C. Price, whose book "How Faith Works," inspired me to enroll in the faith curriculum offered by Crenshaw Christian Center. The study completely changed my life. Thank you, Dr. Price, for living an exemplary life in the Word.

I also honor my mentors in the faith, Dr. Ira Hilliard, Pastor Ron Merthie, Pastor Michael Freeman, Dr. Steve Houpe, Dr. Alfred Harvey, Pastor Greg Powe, Dr. Leroy Thompson, Bishop T.D. Jakes, and Dr. Myles Munroe.

To Bishop Wayne T. and Beverly Jackson, thank you for training up the best intercessor and wife a man could dream of in Jewel.

To my faith buddies, Bishop Alton Williams, Pastor Ron Frierson, Pastor Sherwood Wilson, Prophet Lloyd Bustard, Pastor Greg Hopkins, Dr. Alex Alexander, Pastor Rodney Beard, Pastor Herb Rowe, Pastor Elliot

Shepherd, Pastor James Pierce, Pastor David Forbes and Bishop Terry Hornbuckle, I say "Thank You" for always being there.

To my sons in the ministry, keep up the good work as you lead your flocks to the promise land
.

Thank you, to the faithful members of our church, Destiny Center, for your prayers and for covering your pastor. And thanks to Verity Records, my recording label. You are that important vessel God has used to share my music to the entire world. Thank you for allowing me to be me.

To Wayman Tisdale, A.C. Green, and Darryl Green for being an encouragement to me over the years and for also letting their lights of anointing shine in the NBA and NFL.

Thank you to all of my family, friends, extended family, industry supporters, sponsors and partners for being part of my testimony.

www.Faith-It-Til-You-Make-It.com

Table of Contents

Introduction

Expectation is the breeding ground for a miracle. As one of the most successful Christian instrumental artists of all time, it is easy to assume that Ben Tankard was born with a silver spoon in his mouth. Considering the huge mansion he calls home, the fancy cars, private plane and limo, and even the fact that capacity crowds fill "The Minstrel's" concerts and speaking engagements, it is easy to understand why.

The fact is, that cannot be further from the truth.

In this inspiring book, Ben reveals the gut-wrenching true story of a life living in abject poverty, and obstacles that included divorce and death that faced him on his way to achieving success. His story exposes the pain behind the passion and how, despite his God-given talent, he did not step into the increase of God's favor on his life until he began to put God first and live a consistent life based solely on the Word of God. Today, Ben's life and walk of faith has totally transformed him and his family into vessels that are used daily by God.

As you explore these pages, you will learn about that transformation through Ben's own personal testimony. You will also learn some of the biblical principles he applied to bring about a change in his life and raise him out of a pit of poverty and despair and into a life of faith, prayer and prosperity.

While we encourage you to read Ben's personal testimony, then proceed through this book, be advised that each chapter stands alone and does not have to be read in any particular order. So feel free to go directly to the chapter that fits your situation and find your answers.

We pray that this testimony and these teachings will inspire and encourage you to begin a life that has God at its center. If you do, the best is yet to come!

—*Jewel Tankard*

www.Faith-It-Til-You-Make-It.com

Chapter 1

From Test to Testimony
The Call of a Minstrel

To those familiar with me, I'm known simply as "Ben" or "Minstrel." But when I was born on January 10, 1964 in Daytona Beach, Fla., my parents named me Benjamin Lee Tankard. "Benjamin" came from the Bible. My father, Elder Arthur Tankard, was a Pentecostal preacher and my mother, Mary, was an evangelist. We were part of the Church of God in Christ.

They are both in heaven now, but I really thank God for my parents. They were tough on me as I was growing up, and boy am I glad they were.

Church was always a big part of our lives. I can remember those early years when we were so active in church. There was always something going on.

Sundays were always taken up with the normal Sunday school and morning worship services. But then it seemed like there was always something happening every Sunday evening. If it wasn't a choir anniversary, there was YPWW (Young People Willing Workers) or some other "special" service. And then there were the evening services.

On Monday the Pastor's Aide Society met; Tuesday there was Bible Study; Wednesday was the day for the home and foreign missions meetings; Thursday was choir rehearsal; and on Friday night there was another service. Saturday was sometimes a free day, but only if there was not a church car wash or fish or chicken dinner sale scheduled.

I was in church every day of the week!

As a result of our strict church life, my parents were very strict regarding our lifestyles. My two sisters were not allowed to wear pants (I can remember them swimming in jean skirts), and we had very little involvement with anyone or anything outside of our church circle.

That meant we never went to the movies.

In addition to the rigorous church schedule, we also acknowledged Saturday as the Lord's Day (just in case the Sunday worshippers were wrong and the Roman calendar was off.). You can imagine how much more confined that made my two sisters feel and me. We already had no outside activities. It was church, church, church, all the time! And now there was no television or playing games on Saturday—The Sabbath!

At the time, it seemed like being in prison. But in reality, it was just a set-up for a step up!

Little Drummer Boy

When I was three years old, I began banging on my mother's pots and pans. I don't know what prompted me into an early life of destruction, but I just liked banging on pots and pans. At any rate, my mother liked what she saw (and heard for that matter) and realized pretty fast that she had a little drummer boy on her hands.

I can remember wishing for a drum every year when Christmas rolled around. But we were poor. Very poor! Many of our clothes came from the Goodwill, and many of the Christmas presents we received came from the Salvation Army.

One Christmas when I was seven years old, my school had try-outs for a Christmas production of "The Little Drummer Boy." I didn't own a snare drum like the other boys who auditioned for the part, but my mother decided to take me to try out anyway. When I stepped to the stage to audition, my teacher noticed I didn't have a drum. Rather than embarrass me in front of the others by reminding my mother that having a snare drum was required, the teacher had one of the other students set up his drum for me to use. About halfway through my audition, the teacher stopped me and said: "We do not need to proceed any further. This young man is who we are looking for."

The Christmas play took place later that week, and I was excited as I stood proudly in the place of the "Little Drummer Boy." To my delight, though I was probably too young to soak it all in, I received standing ovations for my performance. After the play, the teacher surprised me by giving me the snare drum she had purchased for use in the play. It was the most expensive thing I had ever owned in my entire life. She also said how proud she was that I not only performed well, but that my mother had dressed me so perfectly for the part I played.

She had no idea that I was not dressed ragged on purpose. She never knew that the clothes I wore that night, an old tattered shirt and some cut off blue jeans, were some of my "normal" clothes. I remember my Mom testifying in church about how the torn clothes had been a "blessing in disguise" and how God used them to make a way for her son to have a drum.

I was proud of that little drum, and would carry it to most of the church services we attended. I would set it up and play during devotion services (what we now call Praise and Worship service). God was using me at a young age.

Reality of Poverty!

It was also during this time that I took a strong liking to reading. I had a serious stuttering problem and did not speak much in public. I had to take speech therapy at school twice a week. So reading was a good way to spend my time.

Since it was free, my sisters and I would spend a lot of time in the public library. I averaged reading about five to seven books a week. My mother jokingly referred to me as "The Doctor" because she thought it odd that a child so young would read as many as 25 books a month. She did not realize it at the time, but my mind and intellect were being prepared for greatness.

My mother never really worked outside the home. We children kept her plenty busy. As for my father, he loved us and did his best to provide for us. His options were limited, though, because he left school at a very early age. His primary income came from collecting beer cans on the beach near where we lived. We helped, and usually got an allowance of 10 cents each week.

My father drove an old station wagon, which he used to dump the cans he collected. He would leave home around 4 o'clock each morning to collect cans and return late in the evening, usually with the entire passenger and storage sections of the station wagon piled high with beer cans.

Imagine the stench. But it didn't seem to bother my father, whose focus was on providing for his family.

And talk about nasty! Sometimes there would be so many cans piled inside that car that all you could see was my father's head as he drove up to the house. He would dump the cans in our backyard and go for another load. This would happen all day until around sundown. Usually, we had a mountain of cans in the back yard by the end of the day.

My mother would supervise as my sisters and I smashed the cans and packed them into recycle bags. Sometimes, there would be bugs and snails crawling around those cans. Every now and then a snake would crawl out from one and scare us. We were a close-knit, loving family and, though times were hard, we stuck together and always tried to make the best of things despite the circumstances.

That's how we spent our summers. Come to think of it, that is pretty much how we spent most of the year, even when we were in school. Smashing cans for two hours before going to school, then another four or five hours after coming home, and finally cramming them inside plastic bags so my father could take them to the recycling center for money.

It was his sole source of income.

"What a way to grow up," I used to think. Not that I was critical of my parents. They always took care of us. But I just didn't understand why it was just so hard to have food or a decent place to live. Now that I'm all grown up, I understand some things. I understand that my parents were living under what is described as a "generation curse" of poverty. They were the sweetest, most loving parents in the world.

The church we attended did not preach prosperity, so we didn't know how to exercise faith for what we wanted. We didn't have enough faith to believe past where we were. The Bible says faith comes by hearing and hearing by the Word of God (Romans 10:17). But we never heard it preached consistently that we could prosper, therefore we never prospered. In fact, I remember that the only time we ever set any family goals to get ahead was when we went shopping at the local trailer park. We really began to dream when we would look at those big doublewides!

We were on welfare, which meant we got food stamps and government "rations" that usually included powdered eggs, powdered milk, peanut butter in a big silver can, and big blocks of cheese.

When prices for recycling went down, so did my father's income. For a while, he worked as a janitor at a motel. Then later he became a migrant worker. Sometimes, he would be gone for weeks at a time, depending on what crops were being harvested. He was a very hard worker.

My father also spent a lot of time praying and fasting. We had a freestanding garage that he had converted into a prayer room. Every evening after dinner he would make his way to that prayer room where he would spend time praying, reading and talking to God. Sometimes, the neighbors could hear him out there praying at night.

Start of Something—New?

One time, my father took on some migrating work that kept him away from the family for a number of weeks. When he returned, he shared the news that he had found steady work with a sod company in Starke, Fla. He also said he had found a building in Starke and would be starting a church.

You can imagine the excitement among us children, and our mother. It meant a fresh start at life. No more poverty. No more welfare, food stamps and government cheese. It was an exciting time for the Tankard family. I was ready for prosperity!

Then we arrived in Starke.

It was in August of 1975. I was 12, and very tired of

work and church.

But what we found in Starke was a far, and I do mean far cry from what we had expected. The place we were to live was in Reno, the roughest, most crime and drug-infested area of the city. Our "new" home was not a house at all. It was a tiny apartment in back of an old abandoned movie theater built in the 1950s. The building had a musty odor, signifying it had not been used in years.

The neighborhood kids were pretty hard on us, too. Often, they shunned us and poked fun at the way we dressed and the place we lived. "Hey, Tankard, what's playing at the movies tonight?" they would say, alluding to our home being an old theater.

We were a laughing stock. But it was a set-up for a step-up!

Our clothes still came from the Goodwill, and our daily meals consisted mainly of chicken backs and turkey butts that my mother would buy at the local meat market for 10 cents a pound.

Often, my father would have to leave to work in the fields. We had no telephone, and for a while there was no television to keep us company. Shortly after we moved to Starke, my father started his church, Revival Temple, in that old abandoned theater. We did not have many members, and many days it was my family that made up the congregation.

Despite that, but God was faithful. It was a learning experience for us all.

Soon, short trips turned into long ones for my father and he was gone for months at a time doing migrant work. While on the road, he often ran church revivals. That meant he was away from home for even longer periods of time. I loved my father, and would often lay in bed and cry because I missed him so much when he was gone. One of my fondest memories was when he taught me to fly a kite. My father was the world's best kite flyer. He could make a kit fly on a day when there was no wind!

We missed out on a lot of father and son events. My father never even got a chance to see me play in a basketball game because he was crippled by lack and was always trying to make ends meet.

I remember thinking that I wanted a better life when I grew up. I also remember how determined I was to do something about the situation to make life better for my mother and my sisters immediately. My dad loved us. I knew that. And he was doing all he could to provide. But I wanted more – for them and for myself.

My two sisters, Patrice and Avalier, were the joy of my life. Patrice was a year older than me and Avalier was a year younger. They took real good care of me. And I returned the favor.

They always kept me encouraged. And, unlike most siblings, we didn't fight a lot. Most of our fighting was against the rats and roaches that infested our "home." Patrice was very gifted musically. She played piano and sang. Ava sang. We once had a group called "Sister Tankard and the Tankardetts." It was fun! We sang at most of the local church functions, and surprisingly were very popular.

One of my odd jobs was catching chickens and shoveling manure on a poultry farm. The smell of chicken manure is somewhat similar to the awful spray of a skunk. It doesn't wash off easily, so sometimes that odor would linger on my body. I also had a rather large head for my size. The neighborhood kids took advantage of those two things, and would get fun out of calling me names like Tanka Stank, Water Head, Headquarters and PRE (short for prehistoric dinosaur). I may not have looked or dressed like I stepped out of *G.Q.* magazine, but I certainly didn't deserve that kind of treatment. People can be very cruel.

A Return to Music

When I reached middle school, my attention immediately turned to music. I wanted to play trumpet, but the band director took one look at my big lips and decided I was born to play tuba. Within three weeks, I was in advance band, and six weeks later I was playing in the high school concert band—despite the fact that I was only in the seventh grade. By the time I reached high school I was playing in the University of Florida's Symphony Orchestra. I won All-American honors as a tuba player and was voted the No. 3 tuba player in the nation.

That same year, I tried out for and excelled in basketball. My six foot, five-inch frame came in pretty handy on the basketball court.

Despite the triumphs and successes in school, poverty was still a real-life situation in my family. And I needed to do something about it.

I went to work as a dishwasher at a nearby barbecue restaurant called Sonny's Bar-B-Q. We lived about five miles from Sonny's, so transportation was no problem. I rode my bicycle to and from work. Sometimes I worked late, but no matter how late it was when I got home my mother and sisters would always wait up for me. I would always try to have some sort of treat for them from the restaurant like pie, cake, or banana pudding.

When I was 15, my father was still away for months

at a time working and I found myself having to play the role of "father" and "provider."

The following year my older sister got married and moved back to Daytona Beach. I envied her because I wished it were me leaving. Though I had a good attitude and learned to bare poverty and disappointment with a smile, there was something on the inside of me that always despised lack.

It was nothing short of a miracle that I had time to study because of work, but yet I maintained a "B" average in every one of my classes.

At work, I eventually moved up to short-order cook. That meant more money, which meant I was now in a better position to help support the family. At age 15, I was supporting the family, holding down a job, involved in band and basketball in school, and still managing to keep up my grades. Things began to get a little better and God blessed us to be able to shop at K-Mart and eat out sometimes. My dad had found work with a sod company in South Florida. I still missed him terribly but life was finally looking up for the Tankards.

Then tragedy struck.

One day when I was away from home a couple from South Florida came to the house looking for my mother. The minister and his wife said they were neighbors of my father. When my mother looked inside the couple's car, she saw my father lying in a crumpled heap on the back seat. The couple said they had found my dad, near death, lying on the floor inside his rundown apartment. He had not eaten in weeks and had developed a serious infection in his hip. He had refused medical treatment, they said, and appeared to be paralyzed.

My mother rushed my dad to the hospital, where doctors performed surgery to remove a large portion of his hip. For days and weeks after the surgery, my mom was at my dad's side, nursing him and seeing after his every need. I was nervous and scared about his condition but I buried my anxieties in my schoolwork, my basketball, and band.

After spending a few months recovering, my dad was back on his feet and back at work doing odd farming jobs around town. It wasn't exactly the kind of work we wanted him to be doing, but at least it kept him busy. And, it kept him at home. Finally, it looked like our lives were gravitating to some degree of normality.

More tragedy struck when my mother's mom died a few months later. My mother was devastated.

Grandma lived in a small town about 30 miles from Tallahassee called Chattahoochee. When we went to the funeral, we learned that my grandmother had left her family home to my mother. It was a two-bedroom "shotgun" wooden country house (complete with a wood-burning stove). But it was clean and paid for.

The summer before my senior year in high school, my mom, my baby sister and I moved to Chattahoochee. My father found a job working in a plant at Lake Butler, Fla., a small town about 18 miles from Starke, so he had to stay behind to make money. I was happy to be leaving Starke and happy that my father had a consistent job. But I was sad that we were going to be separated again.

A New Beginning—A Very Small Town

Chattahoochee was much smaller then Starke.

In the entire town there were only two traffic lights. The high school, Chattahoochee High, was on Chattahoochee Street. And the only fast-food restaurant in town was appropriately called Chattaburger.

I got a job at the Chattaburger, but quit after the first week when I learned I was making "minimum wage" of $1.50 an hour. No one had to tell me it had something to do with the fact that I was black. Chattahoochee was very backwards. And somewhat racist.

It was 1982, and this town still had separate proms for the black and white kids!

But racism seemed to show up only where the town's people wanted it to be seen. For instance, the basketball team at Chattahoochee High was horrible. Their record the prior season was a pitiful 0-26. Needless to say, the coaches were glad to see my six-foot, five-inch frame show up in the registrar's office, despite the fact I was black.

Because my mom had inherited a small amount of money from my grandmother, along with the shotgun row house, we were pretty much debt free. Our only monthly expenses were utility bills, which totaled about $28 a month, and food. Not having to work freed me up to concentrate on my school studies, band and basketball. I had an exciting year filled with major accomplishments.

The year I played on the basketball team we won almost 20 games, and I was considered a star player. I also excelled in band. Between basketball and band, I was offered more than 23 scholarships during my senior hear. I accepted a basketball scholarship to Wallace State in nearby Alabama, reasoning that I could get plenty of playing time in basketball and still be close enough to home that I could visit my family on weekends.

The biggest part of my plan, though, was that after college I would play professional basketball. I got as far as basketball camp, as a walk-on, and almost immediately I got injured. My hopes of playing professional ball were dashed in an instant. And almost as instantly I found myself back in poverty. This is where my life really began to take a turn for the worse. With no money or contract I was back where I had started as a child… poverty level.

On top of that, a pride issue had developed with me. I had gained a degree of popularity in Chattahoochee, having been voted "Most likely to succeed" my senior year in high school and all. The city of Chattahoochee was counting on me. I couldn't return to Florida a failure.

Before long, I found myself living in the confinement of a little mobile home duplex in Dothan, Alabama with no electricity or water. It was 10 degrees below zero, and I had no food to eat. I felt like I was literally at the brink of death!

Up until then, I had abandoned church life and was living life "my way" as "Old Blue Eyes" Frank Sinatra used to sing. I never had any vices to speak of, like smoking, drinking or doing drugs. But I had pretty much put the Church and Jesus Christ out of my life.

A Real Turning Point

Things had gotten progressively bad for me and there was no sign of a turnaround. I was desperate for sure. And as the old saying goes: "Desperate people do desperate things."

Desperate for me was turning back to God.

One night I decided to attend a revival service at a nearby Church of God in Christ. Little did I know that that night would bring an experience that would change my life forever. As the service neared an end the minister gave an altar call, inviting people to give their lives to Christ. I was raised in a Christian environment, and had spent most of my life in the church. But I don't know that I can honestly say that I had ever taken a step toward salvation.

That night, at that service, I did. I received Christ that evening as Lord of my life, and I was baptized with the Holy Spirit (Ghost). But something else happened to me that evening.

When the minister anointed my head and hands with oil, he instructed me to go sit down at the organ. I had never seriously played piano or organ before in my life. But that night, under the mighty power of the Holy Ghost, I began to play like a seasoned professional!

It was the most amazing thing I had ever experienced. Sounds were coming from that organ that neither I, nor anybody else in that room, had ever heard. They were beautiful sounds. Anointed sounds! Somehow I knew the sounds were from God. I knew that I had been anointed with a special gift.

Today, I call that gift God gave me "Gospel Jazz."

The next few years for me were like a roller coaster ride. I moved back to Florida for a while, living in Tallahassee. I made some good career decisions, and I made a few bad ones. But God always showed me mercy.

My fathers health began to fail again and he was no longer able to work, so he came home for good. Being in Tallahassee, which was about 30 minutes from Chattahoochee, made it easy for me to be able to visit with my family.

In college, I studied criminology and for a while after school was a private detective. Somehow, the idea of a six-foot, five-inch tall black man following a white man around trying to catch him cheating on his wife was not very attractive, or lucrative. So, that career was very short-lived. I also tried my hand at being an animal control officer (dogcatcher). But for some reason I knew God had something more He wanted me to do than playing in churches on Sundays for $25 or "arresting" dogs during the week.

One day I was hanging out at a local music store and trying out some of the keyboards when the owner came up and complimented me on my playing skills. He then offered me a job in the store as a keyboard demonstrator. Glory to God! Suddenly, I was going to get paid to do what I enjoyed—playing music. And I would get to do it all day!

The job paid the same as my dogcatcher job, so I was not losing anything by switching "professions." Plus, I got to work indoors.

One day I was demonstrating a keyboard when a customer asked if I knew any classical music. Obviously, I was not trained in classical music. What we learned in band never crossed over into the ritzy, classical realm. But for some reason I answered "yes." When I sat down to demonstrate on a keyboard the customer was interested in buying, the miraculous happened. I put my hands on the keys and sounds came out that would make Bach or Beethoven smile. Seriously!

I was playing serious classical music and had never had any training!

It was God, and I knew it!

Needless to say, the customer liked what he heard and bought the keyboard. From that point on, classical and music was a big part of my demonstration (as well as jazz and gospel music). That incident set the precedent for my demonstrations from that point on.

Before long, I was making enough money to start buying music equipment. I set up a music studio in my home and started making demonstration music tapes for others and myself. At Benote Studios, a person could pay $25 to $50 and record two songs.

On My Own

I began developing my own playing skills and producing my own unique style. Two people came to be very special in my life during that time— ministers Kenneth and Helena Barrington. They "adopted" me as their "music-son" and constantly prophesied and poured into my life. They were also my very best customers at Benote.

Mom Barrington, as I called her, was an anointed writer of praise and worship songs and prophetic music. They would usually spend as much as $500 to $700 per month in studio work. The Lord blessed me to have a number of faithful customers, mainly white, who came into the studio every week to record their work. Being exposed to their music helped me to develop my skills in areas other than black gospel music.

After working in the business for about three years, I saw some fruit from my labor when one of the albums I produced, a record by gospel saxophonist Allen "T.D." Wiggins, became popular nationally. Wiggins went on to team with pianist Bruce Allen and formed a duet called Allen and Allen, but for a while the two of us traveled the gospel music circuit together. I played keyboards.

The Lord began to give me songs in my dreams, and I would get up in the middle of the night and record them in my home studio. Soon, I had enough songs to record an album. "All Keyed UP," my very first album, was born right there in my living room on an eight-track recording system.

It was a major accomplishment. Or at least I thought so. There would be enough people out there to convince me otherwise. Satan had them waiting.

I began sending out demos of my music, certain that people in the music industry would be as excited as I was about this new sound God had given me called "Gospel-Jazz."

Not so.

The negative responses poured in like rain. To secular companies, my music was "too gospel." The gospel music people said it was "too jazzy." Some of the demo tapes were even returned unopened and stamped "Unsolicited Material." It was a perfect opportunity to fall deep into depression and drop the whole idea of becoming a musician. After all, if the music experts were telling me my stuff was no good, where else was there to go?

I decided to use another tactic. I sent my tape to duplication company and had 500 copies made at a cost of 70 cents per tape. My plan was to sell them to the people in my church, and other churches in the area. At $10 each, I could have $5,000 in no time.

Turned out that was not as easy as I had thought, either.

Nobody wanted the tapes. Not even the folk from my own church. When time came to go to the annual Church of God in Christ Convention in Memphis, I still had 484 tapes packed away in boxes.

I carried the tapes with me to the convention, thinking surely a majority of the 75 church members on the Greyhound bus we rode to the convention on would want to support a fellow church member and buy a tape.

I sold one tape! Others were too busy voicing their opinions about the music.

"That's too jazzy," one person said. "Nobody wants that ugly music," was the opinion of another. Talk about discouraged. With only $12 in my pocket, I had to do something.

Breakthrough—Not a Moment Too Soon!

One of the reasons for carrying my tapes to the convention was that I had heard that vendors could set up booths and sell merchandise. I didn't have any money to pay for a booth. But surely, I thought, someone would let me peddle my wares alongside theirs. I could pay them from my profits.

No one was interested.

One man I spoke with was also selling gospel music. He listened to my proposal, but refused to give up any space in favor of keeping it for his own merchandise. He did offer me a job helping to sell his merchandise. But he wanted me to come back near the end of the week. He felt business would pick up by then.

Then, he asked ME for a favor. He wanted me to watch his booth while he went to the restroom.

While he was gone, I decided to put on one of my tapes in a stereo he had set up in his booth. Within minutes, people were crowding around the booth with questions about the music that was playing and wanting to buy a copy of "All Keyed UP."

By the time the vendor returned to his booth, I had sold out of the 30 tapes I brought to the booth. I made $300 in about 10 minutes.

Almost immediately, he offered to let me use his booth to sell my tapes if I would give him $3 from every tape I sold. He kept my music playing while I went to get the rest of the more than 400 tapes and we were in business. In no time at all we had sold out. And we both had made a nice size piece of money.

Surprisingly, among the curious standing in the crowd were some people I recognized. My church members! The very people who had called my music "too jazzy," and said nobody wanted "that ugly music."

There they stood, bragging that they knew me and that I was "one of theirs."

The following year, I began traveling to all the major church conventions where I would rent my own booth and sell my music. It paid handsomely. Not only was I making some money but also I was finally building a fan base that would help when my music went national.

In early 1989, I received a call from Atlanta International Records (AIR) in Atlanta expressing interest in distributing my music to the gospel and jazz markets. From the beginning, the project raised a few eyebrows but God blessed it and before long radio stations were using my music as filler, and as background music during prayer time and announcements. I was being played on hundreds of stations every hour around the clock, which quickly got the ears of radio announcers.

There were a number of other things that transpired that would take another whole book to explain. But the important thing is that God began to work in my life and before long I found myself traveling around the country, introducing Gospel-Jazz music and sharing my testimony of how God transferred me from a basketball team to HIS team.

Finally, after years of struggle, I had attained.

It was not easy. And when I look back, I know more than ever that it had to be a mighty, powerful God to bring me to the place I find myself today.

I made many mistakes along the way.

At age 22, I rushed into a marriage without Godly counsel only to have that marriage dissolve away in divorce. I also got bad advice from a former manager that led to near financial ruin.

But some decisions I made were good ones, like my decision to seek the opinion of others in the business by sending them copies of "All Keyed UP." I must have given away 1,000 copies of that tape. But it proved to be worth it.

One day I received a call from a man in Nashville who identified himself as vice president of a top gospel music distributing company. He liked my music and wanted to find a way to help get it distributed. A month later, he introduced me to the president of Diadem Music, a contemporary Christian music label in Nashville. George King, the president, also liked my music and wanted to offer me a chance to come work for him as a vice president of a newly created Black division that would be called Tribute Records.

I accepted, and relocated to Nashville.

Regretfully, I moved so quickly that I failed to properly end my relationship with Alan Freeman and AIR, the ones responsible for giving me my first big break. That's something I will always be sorry about, even though we are still friends and have the best of relationships. (Caution! Always make sure you handle your affairs in the proper order. Integrity in relationships is key to success. You don't want to have to learn that the way I did.)

The move to Nashville, and my position as a vice president of a record company, opened a lot of doors for me to work with, sign and produce music for a number of artists who went on to become recognized celebrities. One of those was Yolanda Adams, who signed her first record deal with Tribute. She had been a featured performer on Southeast Inspiration Choir's early recordings and had recorded a regionally received debut release with the late Thomas Whitfield.

She was a monster talent with untapped potential.

After signing Yolanda, we recorded six records together for Tribute. She won awards for each of them.

I was also blessed to work with Twinkie Clark, Take 6, Fred Hammond, John P. Kee, Angie and Debbie Winans, and a number of other gifted singers while working with Tribute as my career started an upward spiral of its own. I recorded a number of hits that garnered the prestigious Stellar Award for gospel music, including songs like "Keynote Speaker," "Keys to Life," "Play Me In Your Key," "Sunday Drivin'," "Instrumentally Yours," "Instrumental Christmas," and "Ben Tankard & Tribe of Benjamin."

Along the way I wrote the song and coined the phrase "Git Yo Prayze On," a phrase that was quickly adopted by such gospel music artists as Kirk Franklin, Fred Hammond and Donald Lawrence and Men of Standard. What an honor! My songs won me nine Stella Awards and I received eight Dove and three Grammy nominations. I became the best-selling Gospel Jazz instrumentalist of all time. And it was all because of God.

I wanted to be a basketball player. God just wanted a player. And He chose me.

Consult the Life Changer—First!

At 35, I had already experienced four major changes in my life. In closing this chapter, I want to share them with you.

First, was that night in Alabama when I met Jesus Christ. I was lost and confused with nowhere to turn. And a loving God wrapped His arms around me, anointed me with His love and His power, and saved me. Then, He gave me the gift to play music.

The second experience came after a trip I made to the Holy Land in 1997. It was there that the Lord showed me that my destiny was not just that of an anointed Minstrel but that I was called to pastor.

Shortly after returning from the Holy Land, I made preparations to enter Bible School. I studied faith, healing, prosperity and the Holy Spirit. And as I did so, the Word and the miracles of Jesus became real to me. My faith for these things increased, and I began to see them manifest in my life. When I played during concerts, people were healed. People in wheelchairs got up and walked. Tumors dropped off and ulcers melted away!

The Lord began to show me all the benefits of salvation that resulted from being obedient to His Word and walking in my calling. He moved me to put into practice the things He was showing me.

The third life-changing event happened in 1998 during a conference I was attending led by Dr. Creflo A. Dollar Jr. My spiritual parents in the Lord, Dr. Rick and Sis. Barbara Layton of Shreveport, La., had invited me to the conference.

I ministered in song from the piano that night and the anointing of God was really strong. Following a stirring message by Dr. Leroy Thompson, Pastor Dollar called me to the platform where he anointed me, then spoke words of prophecy. As I yield to God, he said, I would be raised up as a "spiritual Pied Piper" (like

David) to usher people into God's presence and speak out against the spirit of the Hireling and other perversions that had invaded the Christian music arena. He also said a major change was about to happen in my life. He laid hands on me and imparted a spirit of increase.

That marked an immediate change in the way I conducted my business affairs. From that day until now, I have never charged a fee for any of my concerts or public appearances. I began a walk of faith that went against the grain of the gospel music industry, asking only for lodging and travel expenses. A love gift was, and still is today, totally at the discretion of the host.

I live by faith, putting pressure on the Word of God (not people) and the Lord has always provided. In many cases, my love gifts have turned out to be more than what I would have required under a contract.

Before long, I was being booked for over 150 concerts a year!

I remember when I assembled the Tribe of Benjamin to record the "Git Yo Prayze On" album. We had no viable means of transportation to move a team of 14 people, so we rented a nice, comfortable tour bus that was large enough to accommodate the entire crew. When I realized just how much money we were putting out in rental charges, I decided to trust God for a bus of our own.

To exercise my faith for that bus, I hired a painter to come to our office and paint a 50-foot parking space in front of my recording studio. I then put up a sign that read: "Tour Bus Parking."

When the painter asked when I was expecting delivery on the bus, I looked toward heaven and responded: "Any day now." Within two weeks, I received a call from a tour company saying they had a "return" from a country music artist who ordered a custom coach but then decided to buy a plane instead. They told us to come and get the bus, and not to be concerned about a bank loan to pay for it. We could pay them when we got the money, they said.

We dedicated that bus to the Lord and named it "The Prophecy."

Another time, I spoke to the Lord about my personal financial situation. I asked Him to send me money everyday. He responded by leading me to Galatians 6:7 *"God is not mocked, whatsoever a man soweth, that he shall also reap."*

The revelation I received was that if I wanted to "receive" money everyday, then I needed to "give" money everyday. So, I put that into practice. Everyday, I would put a financial offering of some amount in the mail to a particular ministry. The gifts ranged anywhere from $1 to $1,000, but regardless of the amount I was consistently sending that offering everyday.

It wasn't long before God honored His Word and started giving back to me.

Within 90 days, my family had been supernaturally blessed with increase, including a 7,000-square-foot home, a Navigator truck, an S-series Mercedes and SUV, a boat and a motorcycle. The tour bus was sold, and today we are on our third airplane! We call it "The Manifestation".

I give everyday, and I receive everyday. It is so simple.

There were some hardships along the way.

I lost both my parents to sickness within a 14-month period. During that time I was also going through a divorce. It seemed that while increase was coming in one form, I was losing in others.

Through fasting and prayer, God strengthened me.

The fourth life-changing event that has totally impacted my life took place when I attended a prophetic conference in Detroit and laid eyes on God's appointed "Esther" for my life. Her name is Jewel and she is God's perfect will as my wife.

Together, we make beautiful music. An anointed woman of God, she is everything I know God intended a man to have. And I cherish her deeply.

In addition to our music ministry, and her career as a businesswoman, fashion model and speaker, we pastor The Destiny Center, one of the fastest-growing churches in Tennessee. We also share the joys of a blended family with children from our previous marriages.

It's Waiting for You!

Everyone can be anointed. Everyone can be appointed. Everyone can be healed, delivered and set free from the snares of financial ruin. I know. I have been there. If you can wake up you can look up. If you can look up you can get up. If you can get up you can get going!

My desire is to inspire others, and especially musicians and singers, to strive to do all that you do for the Lord. If you are a musician, become a minstrel for the Lord. If you are called to sing, become His Psalmist.

I did not prosper because I was a good keyboard player. No, I walk in prosperity and the blessings of the Lord because I obey what He tells me. I have a hold on His Word and I won't let it go.

Get a hold of His Word. Hold tight and never let go. Let it work for you like it has worked for me and countless others who have dared to trust God.

If we can make it, so can you! Your test will become testimonies!

www.Faith-It-Til-You-Make-It.com

40

Chapter 2

Faith It—'til You Make It!
The Winning Formula for Faith

I have a couple of questions for you and I want you to answer honestly. No one is around to judge you. It's just the two of us, so you're free to be "real" with your answer.

Are you successful and experiencing increase in every area of your life? Are you living the disciplined life of a Christian—treating people right, loving your neighbor, praying everyday and doing all the things you know to do—but still not experiencing the level of success you desire?

In other words, are you broke, busted and disgusted? Are you stuck between the *AMEN* and the *THERE IT IS*? Are you tired of faking it?

If so, then perhaps your faith needs a tune up.

Maybe it is time you started to "Faith It," and not just fake it!

As a believer, it's likely you have heard teaching on the subject of faith many times. You may even be thinking 'I know all there is to know about faith.' Well, let me stop you right there!

The truth is you can never know everything there is to know about faith. Why? Because the Bible says that faith cometh by "hearing." Some like to extend that verse to say that faith comes by "hearing, and hearing and hearing." That's because we never stop hearing. I've heard it said that repetition is the mother of better learning. In other words, the more we hear a thing, the more we can know about that thing. Faith isn't something we learn or attain overnight. It's a gradual process of learning. And, according to Romans 10:17, it begins with the Word of God.

Why is faith so important in our Christian walk?

Part of the answer is found in Hosea 4:6 *"My people are destroyed for lack of knowledge."* Notice it didn't say people are destroyed for a lack of commitment, or a lack of good works, or a lack of speaking in tongues. No. It says God's people are destroyed, perished, for a "lack of knowledge." Knowledge of what? Knowledge of God's Word and what it says.

Did you know the absolute most important thing for a believer once he accepts Jesus Christ as Savior is to learn to walk by faith? The will of God is NOT automatic in our lives. Not only must we study the Word and learn the inheritance, promises, and blessings we are entitled to, but we should be aware of the curses (like poverty, sickness, and spiritual death) so we will know what to avoid and what not to accept in our lives as "God's will".

For something to truly become a part of us, to become embedded in our spirits and to be the major force of our thought life, we have to constantly renew ourselves by feeding our spirits on the Word. That's what hearing is about. In Romans 12:2, Paul tells us to *"be not conformed to this world: but be ye transformed by the renewing of your mind."* How is the mind renewed? By hearing something over and over and over.

Even the world knows that repetition brings results.

Have you ever noticed, for instance, how easily you can pick up on some secular song just by hearing it over and over on the radio? You're driving along and suddenly you find yourself singing along to some silly song or jingle that's playing. How did you learn those words? Surely, you didn't just sit down and practice until you had them memorized. No. Some way, somehow, that song was introduced into your thinking over a period of time. And subconsciously, you picked up on those words and they became a part of your spirit.

Well, the same principle applies where faith is concerned.

You hear the Word, and you hear the Word, and you hear the Word. And all of a sudden faith in what you have heard begins to grow inside you. The Word becomes just as real as the lyrics to that dumb, silly song you were singing.

This is a spiritual law that will work regardless of how you apply it. If you feed on natural things, you will think natural, carnal thoughts and do natural, carnal deeds. But if you feed your spirit on the things of God— His Word—you will do those things that are in line with His Word.

All things produce after their own kind. A farmer wouldn't plant corn and expect a full crop of beans several weeks down the road. Likewise, a landscape contractor is not going to put out several dozen pounds of grass seed and come back in a few days expecting to see wheat springing up.

In the same manner, you should not expect faith to pop up if you have not planted the proper seed. You won't get a harvest of faith if all you're planting is television soap operas and game shows. When trouble comes and you need to exercise faith to believe, all you'll find coming up out of your spirit is a repeat of what happened on one of those carnal television programs.

As pastors, from time to time we have counseled with people on a variety of subjects. We also know a minister who is very anointed and full of the Word. He did a great job of ministering the Word to his family and leading them in prayer. However, when he was away at work and on business trips his wife would spend all her time reading tabloid magazines, on the phone, watching secular music video shows, and surfing the Internet.

What do you suppose eventually happened to her spiritually? It was not too long before she began acting out some of the story lines she had seen in those soap operas. Because of the sinful ingredients she had constantly fed into her spirit, it wasn't long before she attached herself to the wrong crowd and fell headlong into an extramarital affair. Before long, she was separated, and then divorced. Her family was ripped apart.

Listen, my friends. Your eyes and ears are the "gate" to your heart. The heart is where faith grows. It is your responsibility to GUARD THE GATE!

We are products of our environment. There is no nutritional spiritual value in the things of the world. Just as we need a balanced diet to keep our bodies in good shape, we need to have a balanced diet of the Word. That's where faith begins.

Finding Answers in the Heavens

For me, the word "Faith" has two meanings: "Finding Answers In the Heavens" and "Forsaking All In Trusting Him". As Christians, everything we seek to accomplish has to be done by faith. Everything! Faith is the common thread that connects all the aspects of our spiritual walk with God. Without faith, the scripture says, it is impossible to please God.

The more you hear the Word, the more your trust and confidence in the Word becomes. Faith comes alive in you.

Jesus said if any man have ears to hear, let him hear.

"And he said unto them, Take heed what ye hear: with what measure ye mete, it shall be measured to you: and unto you that hear shall more be given" (Mark 4:24).

The Amplified Bible makes it even clearer: "And he said unto them, be careful what you are hearing. The measure (of thought and study) you give (the truth you hear) will be the measure (of virtue and knowledge) that comes back to you, and more (besides) will be given to you who hear.

Can you see that? Feeding your faith on the Word requires discipline. But in the end that discipline, that time you spent hearing, will pay off. The reason many Christians have problems when it comes to exercising faith is that they are undisciplined. They don't want to take the time to study the Word, or to hear the Word—the things necessary to develop their faith. Their fellowship with God is "hit and miss." Most would rather be doing something more fun—or more self-serving.

Just think of the amount of time you spend on yourself—on the flesh—buying clothes, choosing makeup and hairstyles. All the things that Jesus said profit nothing. Then consider how much time you actually spend in the Word of God. How much time you spend praying? How much time you devote to communion with God?

Is there a balance? Probably not.

And there will also be no faith when it is needed. Why? Because you have not spent the proper time in the Word to build yourself up. You have exchanged your time with heavenly things for those things of the world—the things that profit you nothing.

John 6:63 says, *"It is the Spirit who gives life; the flesh profits nothing. The words that I speak to you are spirit, and they are life"* (New King James Version). If you expect faith to come alive in you, then you must do what is necessary to have faith.

It is said that it takes at least 21 days of doing something continuously for it to become a habit. What a profitable habit mediating on the Word of God would be!

Faith Is NOW

There is a difference between faith and hope.

Hope looks to the future with an expectancy that something you believe will happen will happen. Faith, on the other hand, is always present. It is always NOW. Faith believes that "whatsoever you believe when you pray you received" NOW. Faith doesn't look to the future. It looks to the now—the present.

"Now faith is the substance of things hoped for, the evidence of things not seen" (Hebrews 11:1).

Don't get me wrong. Hope is good, but that's just the starting point. Hope allows you to have a positive attitude. In other words, hope will let you have a smile on your face even as the ship is going down and sinking. But FAITH will make you ACT! It will make you do something to keep that ship from sinking. It will cause you to find a way to stop up the hole and keep the water from coming in. Faith gives you something to look forward to. Faith brings it to past.

Faith believes with the heart (NOW), and confessing with your mouth (NOW), that you believe you receive whatever it is you desire from God. That is made perfectly clear in Mark chapter 11, verses 23 and 24.

"For verily I say unto you, That whosoever shall say unto this mountain, Be thou removed, and be thou cast into the sea; and shall not doubt in his heart, but shall believe that those things which he saith shall come to pass; he shall have whatsoever he saith. Therefore I say unto you, What things soever ye desire, when ye pray, believe that ye receive them, and ye shall have them."

Notice in verse 23 that the word "say" is mentioned four times, but "believe" appears only once. The revelation here is that you must "say" a thing four more times than you have to believe it. A lot of people are doing a lot of saying, but unfortunately they are not saying in faith. Their saying is not NOW faith, but LATER faith.

Maybe you have heard someone say something like: "I know God is going to bless me"; "My healing is just around the corner"; "My new job is on the way." You may have even repeated these words at one time or another yourself.

These are NOT faith-filled words because they are not spoken in the NOW. They are spoken in the FUTURE. Faith is NOW, and the words that you speak in faith have to be in the NOW. Hope is FUTURE.

Sadly, most people who talk this way are doing so out of ignorance of the Word. They are sincere in what they are saying and believing, but they are sincerely wrong. They don't understand that as long as you believe with your heart and confess with your mouth that your blessing is "just around the corner," that's where your blessing will be—just around the corner. And chances are you'll never make it around the corner and the blessing will never find its way to you.

Having a "just around the corner" mentality is not faith! It's hope. And, to a large degree it is also doubt.

Faith doesn't sit around waiting for blessings that are "just around the corner." No, faith goes out, finds those blessings and brings them right to you—wherever you are. You don't have to wait! Speaking words that put your expectancy in the future ("around the corner") instead of in the *now* is like putting your faith in a waiting mode, or holding pattern. When you get to one corner, your blessings will have moved to the next corner. And they'll continue to move. You'll find yourself chasing your blessings instead of calling them in.

You must align your confession with the NOW, not the later. Change your confession and begin speaking "I believe I have received my blessings NOW, in Jesus name." Agree with what God's Word says.

Since we have been created in the image of God, we must attain results the same way He did—by speaking. In Genesis chapter one, God created the heavens and the earth by speaking faith-filled words. He said: "Let there be light," or as some translators have it "Light be!" He did not say: "One day there will be some lights around here" or "Lights are just around the corner."

It is so ironic that the tongue, which is the very thing that can bless you, can lead to your demise as well. Proverbs tells us *"death and life are in the power of the tongue."* One slip of the tongue can mean defeat when you were headed for victory. Faith-filled words, brought forth by the tongue, are the key to your success. Notice, I said "faith-filled" words and not just words.

Say you are standing in front of an eight-bedroom mansion. The owner hands you a bunch of keys and says: "If you pick the right key on the first try and open the door to this mansion, I will give it to you." Your desire, your need or your sincerity would have nothing to do with whether you get into that mansion now would it? No. All you need to do is pick the right key! If you get it wrong, then you've just locked yourself out of a blessing.

That's what happens to a lot of believers in the body of Christ. They live a lifetime of defeat because they try to use the wrong keys to obtain the blessings of God! Then they get upset when they see people like me and my wife Jewel, Creflo and Taffi Dollar, Leroy and Carolyn Thompson, Fred and Betty Price, Dr. Rick and Barbara Laytan, Kenneth and Gloria Copeland come along and using the "right" keys (faith-filled words) and living in mansions, flying around in their own airplanes, and living virtually debt free.

Listen, God is no respecter of persons. He is a respecter of faith-filled words. He wants the same for all His children, but they have to use the right keys!

Faith Is an Action

Another faith key is your actions. Don't just speak what you believe (if you believe it). Act like you believe it. That means you've got to stop allowing circumstances to dictate the way you conduct yourself. First Corinthians says we "walk by faith, not by sight."

You are not moved by circumstances or situations. You are not moved by what your bank account says. You are not moved by what the doctor says. You are moved by what the Word says. And it is on the Word that you base your actions.

You have to be totally controlled by the Word. Even if you can't see it, believe it anyway. Why? Because the Word says it. Faith is Action!   God is not moved by need, pity, or tears. He is moved only by faith.

Since God does not lie, the safest thing to do is to

just agree with what He says about your situation. That means two things must happen. First, you must study the Word and find out what God says about your situation and agree with Him. Second, you have to confess ONLY what The Word says about your situation.

You may have to separate yourself from family and friends to accomplish one or both of these because of possible negative talk. But the results, for you, will prove well worth it. I like that scripture in Luke 8 where Jesus was preparing to raise the ruler's young daughter from the dead. Everyone around Him was filled with doubt and unbelief and saying things like: "She is already dead, Jesus is too late." Well you know what Jesus did? The Word says *"…and he put them all out."* Hallelujah. Jesus didn't have time for any doubt and unbelief. He cleared the room of all unbelief! There may be some people that you need to "put out" in order for your faith to work.

If so, then put them out. You must "guard the gate"!

Let me give you an example of what I mean here.

I remember when I moved to Nashville from Tallahassee, Fla. It was a monumental move for me because I got away from all the "Nay-Sayers" — those who said I would never make it, that nobody would ever endorse anything called "Gospel-Jazz."

Well, at times it may have looked like they were right. But I wouldn't allow those words to deter me. I kept remembering the words I had heard several strong, faith preachers speak: Faith is Action! I chose to believe the opposite of what it looked like. I chose to believe that if I had faith as a grain of a mustard seed, like Jesus said, then I could ask whatever I would and I would receive it. I believed Mark 11:24: *"What things soever ye desire, when ye pray, believe that ye receive them, and ye shall have them."*

I also refused to dwell among unbelievers, or as the Bible says "in the counsel of the ungodly." Today, I am reaping the blessings from believing in and standing on the promises of God.

I have a thriving worldwide ministry, have recorded 13 successful albums, received nine Stellar Awards, three Grammy Nominations, and been nominated for the Dove Award eight times. God has given me a lovely wife and family, placed us in a beautiful home, given us nice cars to drive, an airplane and a new church building. We also walk in divine health.

How did all of this happen for us? I assure you it had nothing to do with my own abilities. No. It was all God. It was His faithfulness to His Word.

It says in Deuteronomy 28:1: "And it shall come to pass, if thou shalt hearken diligently unto the voice of the LORD thy God, to observe *and* to do all his commandments which I command thee this day, that the LORD thy God will set thee on high above all nations of the earth."

It was through our obedience to that Word, wherein I chose to not just be a hearer, but a doer of the Word.

You can do the same thing.

If you're in need of a financial blessing, then you should be eating, drinking, consuming all that God's Word has to say about prosperity.

"But my God shall supply all your need according to his riches in glory by Christ Jesus (Philippians 4:19)."

If you need healing in your body, find scriptures in the Bible that deal with healing and just camp out there. The book of Proverbs is a good place to hang out for healing scriptures.

"My son, attend to my words; incline thine ear unto my sayings. Let them not depart from thine eyes; keep them in the midst of thine heart. For they are life unto those that find them, and health to all their flesh (Prov. 4:20-21).

Once you find scriptures to support your needs, study them and then stand on them. Then begin to speak the answer, not the problem. If you're sick, begin to see yourself well and start speaking it out of your mouth. If you have bills that need paying and you are looking to God for the money, start saying, "I believe that I receive the money to pay these bills."

Actually, if you are looking to God for the money to pay off certain bills you should already have the checks written out, placed inside stamped envelopes ready to be mailed. Now wait a minute. I didn't say go ahead and mail them. That's not faith. That's foolishness and presumption. If you don't have the money in the bank, then you shouldn't be sending out bad checks. That will land you in somebody's jail.

But you can extend your faith, or, in other words, act on your faith by going ahead and writing the checks—knowing that God is faithful to perform His Word. When the money comes in, then you've got the checks ready to mail.

The same is true in other areas, like buying a new car or finding a new home. If you are extending your faith for a new car, then you should have already picked out that car, test driven it, taken a picture of it and have a blowup of it on the wall in your living room where you can see it all the time.

You should have already priced out the insurance and figured it into your budget.

That's called faith!

When a woman is expecting a baby she does not wait until the baby arrives before she prepares the nursery. She starts preparing as soon as she knows she is pregnant. Well, how do you become "pregnant" spiritually? By digging in the Word of God so you can "conceive" what God truly has for you!

That's called faith in action, or faith with works.

"For as the body without the spirit is dead, so faith without works is dead also (James 2:23).

I know this sounds a little strange folks, but it works. Trust me.

God's Word never fails.

You must begin to act like you believe what you say.

My family and I now experience a rush of "jubilee manifestations" because we posture ourselves to receive from God by action. How do you do that? You start saying NOW that you are a millionaire and that you are debt free. Don't wait for it to happen.

Start declaring NOW that you are never sick but walk in divine health.

A good rule of thumb is to never say what you don't want. Even if you are so broke you can't pay attention, never admit it! Speak the Word, not the current conditions.

We've adopted a family slogan and lifestyle we call "Act Like It!" We act out to the letter whatever we confess. I was on the elevator one day and pushed the button but the elevator door kept coming open and would not go up. Eventually I realized that I was pushing the button for the floor I was on! You have to "push" the button (confess) for the "floor" (area in life) you want to go to, not the "floor" (circumstances) you are on! In other words speak and act where you are going, not where you are currently located. Don't set up a tent in the middle of your problems!

For example, I remember sometime ago when we had been standing on the Word for a bigger house. We decided to pick out the house we wanted and act like it was ours. Everyday, when we would leave our home to go about our daily routines, we would leave early enough to drive by the house we had selected. Once there, we would pull up into the driveway, look at the house, thank God for it, then back out and continue on to our destination. On our return trip home, we would again go by the new house, pull up into the driveway, back out and go home.

This may seem like a fruitless exercise to you, and it was to us at first. But the more we did it the stronger our faith grew. Within 60 days we closed on that house! It was ours, praise the Lord! See, we began to "practice the promise," not rehearse the problem.

We used the same kind of faith in action to pay off debts, buy a custom coach tour bus and recording studio for the ministry, and close on a building for our ministry headquarters and church.

God is no respecter of persons. He will do the same for you as He has done for me and countless others.

"Then Peter opened his mouth, and said, Of a truth I perceive that God is no respecter of persons..." (Acts.10:34).

God will also honor His Word for those who will believe it. He is a covenant God. He always fulfills His end of the Covenant. It is up to you to fulfill your end.

"God is not a man, that he should lie; neither the son of man, that he should repent: hath he said, and shall he not do it? or hath he spoken, and shall he not make it good?" (Numbers 23:18).

Faith Traps that Snare Blessings

I have learned that you don't just stumble onto success. You plan for it. There's an old saying that if you shoot for nothing you'll hit it every time. Well, how about this one: "If you don't know where you are going, any road will do"?

Prepare for success, then expect it.

One strategy I have learned that is really effective is one I call setting faith-building traps. It's a neat little trick that will help to propel you into stronger faith.

The idea is to place books and tracks on such subjects as faith, healing, prosperity, and so on in strategic places in every room of your house—places you know you're bound to pass by at least once during the day. That means you'll always have something to read near the television set, right?

Then, put faith-building tapes in every tape player you have, including the car.

Then, practice getting into the presence of God. Get up 30 minutes early each morning and spend time in prayer and studying the Word. Start a scripture memory system and quiz yourself daily on the Word. That's what David did, remember?

"Thy word have I hid in mine heart, that I might not sin against thee" (Psalms 119:11).

Also, spend quality time in prayer. As we discussed earlier, prayer is the key to hearing from God. It is also essential to your knowing how to prosper and be successful.

"This book of the law shall not depart out of thy mouth; but thou shalt meditate therein day and night, that thou mayest observe to do according to all that is written therein: for then thou shalt make thy way prosperous, and then thou shalt have good success

(Joshua 1:8)."

Learn to feed your spirit man at least three times a day —the same as you do your natural man. Attach certain scriptures and confessions to things that you would normally do. That way you are assured of remembering.

For example, you know you are going to brush your teeth every morning. Why not attach a scripture to that act. *"He that dwelleth in the secret place of the most High shall abide under the shadow of the Almighty (Psalms 91:1)."* This is an easy way of remembering to confess God's protection over yourself and your family at the beginning of each day.

Do the same thing while you're getting dressed.

Put on the armor of righteousness, as it is laid out in the book of Ephesians.

"Stand therefore, having your loins girt about with truth, and having on the breastplate of righteousness; And your feet shod with the preparation of the gospel of peace; Above all, taking the shield of faith, wherewith ye shall be able to quench all the fiery darts of the wicked. And take the helmet of salvation, and the sword of the Spirit, which is the word of God (Ephesians 6:14-17)."

By the time you get in the car you should be so charged up that you are a blessing looking for somewhere to happen.

When you take on this kind of spiritual faith walk, you will turn the tables on Satan and put him on the run. Things will begin to happen *for you* instead of *to you*.

Make your faith work for you everyday of your life. Use it for the little things, like headaches and backaches, as well as the big things, like house payments, car payments, and serious illness.

Jesus himself said that if we had the faith as a mustard seed, we could use it for big things—like speaking to mountains. What is the mountain in your life? I'm sure you have one. Well, it doesn't matter. Your faith in God, and in His Word is more than enough to remove it.

Don't be like those doubters who wait until they're on their deathbeds to even attempt to exercise faith. Disaster is not the time to try and put faith into action. It should have been working in your life long before disaster struck. Calling on God in the face of trouble, when no faith has been exercised beforehand is called desperation.

And desperation does not move God.

"But without faith it is impossible to please him: for he that cometh to God must believe that he is, and that he is a rewarder of them that diligently seek him (Hebrews 6:10)."

Faith is what moves God—faith that is applied by one who has taken the time to study God's Word, then hide His word in their heart and believe it.

The more time you spend in the Word of God, building and strengthening yourself with His Word, the more prepared you are when the enemy tries to pull something over on you. When Satan attacks your body with cancer, and you have spent all your time in the Word and not in soap operas and TV talk shows, then you'll be equipped to ward off that sickness.

Read Psalms 107:20, which says *"He sent his word, and healed them, and delivered them from their destructions"*. Also notice in James 4:7, the Apostle said *"Submit yourselves therefore to God. Resist the devil, and he will flee from you. Draw nigh to God, and he will draw nigh to you."*

You won't hear anything on those soaps and talk shows that you can quote to Satan and make him flee. But you will find something in the Word. And what you find there will be exactly what you need to bring your faith to a level that you can have whatever you say.

Faith cometh by hearing, and hearing by the Word of God.

The Bible says that every man is given *the* measure of faith. How you nurture that faith, how you develop it and how you use it depends on you.

Obey the Laws of Progression
ABC's of faith: A) God can; B) God will; C) God can and will for ME! (It is just a matter of time)

One of the key elements in the faith walk that is often overlooked is the importance of patience. How long you stick to it and discipline yourself will determine whether or not you achieve the desired result. Many times believers do all the right things we have discussed, but they give up right before the blessing shows up. All that speaking and believing and acting on the Word of God went to waste.

Take care to use the testimonies and the success stories recorded here as an "inspiration" and not an "inclination." They are intended to inspire you to walk by faith and dig into the Word for yourself. Don't go out and get into debt by buying a big house, a car or an airplane when you know you cannot afford it. Again I say, that is not faith. It's foolishness! Don't quit your job and think you are ready to live by faith. No. Live by faith and eventually you will be able to quit that job.

In other words, don't attempt the impossible without having rehearsed the possible. To everything there is a process. That process is the law of progression. As a faith baby, you must crawl before you can walk! Embrace the law of progression and the time will go by faster.

Faith is a spiritual muscle that must be developed. No matter how inspired you get watching the "World's Strongest Man" contest on TV, you would never walk into a gym and begin working out using 600-pound weights. That would be foolish. You would hurt yourself.

Likewise, you should not start "working out" with blessings that are too heavy for your faith. Your faith will be severely damaged.

Believe God for the possible before you attempt the impossible. Allow your faith muscles to develop correctly. Pray that you can make your apartment rent payments on time for a year before you try to take on a larger mortgage payment for a house. If you want to "go there," then you first have got to "sow there."

In James 1: 4, we are admonished to "...*let patience have her perfect work, so ye may be perfect and entire, wanting nothing"*

Don't be moved by setbacks. Sometimes, when we're flying to engagements we have delays because of weather conditions. That's a perfect opportunity to get impatient because, as is the case with most people, we want to get there as fast as possible.

But patience is importance. You never know what is happening on the other end of your destination.

In one case, when our flight was delayed, we later learned that had we left when we wanted to we would not have reached our destination because of a hurricane in the area. That, my friend, was a "divine delay."

Delayed gratification does not mean denied

manifestation. The element that separated us from life and death was time. Time can be your friend.

God is working behind the scenes.

There may be times when you are doing all you know to do and nothing seems to be working. During that time just begin to confess that: *"My faith is working, it is just a matter of time."*

There have been times when we were flying at a low altitude and we experienced lots of turbulence. As a young pilot, I've learned some things about flying and altitude. One is that the lower your altitude the rougher the ride. Hot air from the earth meets up with cold air from the sky and creates "pockets."

The solution was to climb to a higher altitude because the higher you go the thinner the air thus the smoother the ride. But you can't just pull up on the yoke and go up from 4,000 feet to 10,000 feet on your own. You have to get on the radio and request permission from the air traffic controller, the boss of the sky.

Sometimes the air traffic controller will immediately respond with permission to climb higher. But many times the response is: "Please Stand By." He didn't say "no." He said "Please Stand By."

Now even though we were in turbulence, and there was a storm, we were told to hold our course and stand by. Sometimes it would seem like hours before we heard from the controller again, but we had to continue to patiently stand by.

Meantime the storm would get so bad we could not see out the windshield. At that point we had to change the way we were flying. Instead of flying by what we saw through the windshield, we now had to fly by the instruments on the panel. These instruments gave us a true heading, direction and speed as well as radar of storm activity ahead. By flying according to the instruments instead of our relying on our vision, we were more accurate in our navigation because the conditions around us were constantly changing.

This is like what happens in the Christian's walk of faith. We walk by faith (the instruments) not by sight (the windshield).

At the same time we were flying by the instruments, I could hear the ATC talking on the radio with other pilots. I was puzzled because he seemed to be ignoring us and talking to everybody else except us. We were the ones in that storm and needed to go higher. Why were we still on standby?

I later learned that when the controller put us on standby, he was looking at a radar screen that not only showed him our plane but all the planes in the sky around us. (Of course we did not see all the other planes, we were flying by the instruments and could see nothing in the "natural" because of the cloud cover and the storms). When the controller told me to stand by, he radioed ahead of us to planes that were over us, in front of us, and beside us to relocate to other sections of the sky.

The standby was to get other planes out of the way so that we could climb higher!

The controller was creating a highway for us in space. Making a way out of no way!

"Please Stand By" does not mean: "No, you don't deserve it." It means hold your course while God works on your behalf. He is working behind the scenes. Hold on to your faith. Time is your friend!

Faith It— 'Til You Make It!

Faith exercises for your "work out"

1. Write the vision: Start small and work your way up by setting 30-day, 90-day, one-year, three-year and five-year faith goals. Give God praise every step of the way no matter how small the victory.

2. Each week, take the family and drive around in neighborhoods where you know you cannot afford to live. Surround yourself with pictures and concepts of a life in increase. If it is not on your mind it is NOT in your future. Very few things in life are a surprise. You must create a lifestyle of expectancy.

3. Schedule at least 30 minutes each day for dreaming.

4. Pray in the Spirit (tongues) at least 30-45 minutes a day. You can break it up into 3-5 10-minute sessions. Turn off the radio on the way to work and pray and give God praise.

5. Walk in forgiveness at all times. Make a commitment to walk in love and never again have another argument with your spouse or anyone else.

6. Give something away every day. If you have to, start with $1 and build up. The more consistent you are the more God will give you to share.

7. Meditate on the Word daily for whatever area of need you have. Do it day and night.

8. Send us your testimonies and pictures. We may include them in a future newsletter.

Frequently Asked Questions on Faith

Q. What is the biblical definition of faith?

A. Faith is grasping the unreality of hope and bringing it into the realm of reality. Hebrews 11:1 says that faith "...is the substance of things hoped for, the evidence of things not seen." This means that when you pray you are 100 percent convinced that you have what you prayed for, regardless of your natural senses.

Q. What is the prayer of faith?

A. In Mark 11:24, the scripture says *"Whatsoever things you desire when you pray, believe that you receive them and you shall have them."* This is praying the prayer of faith. You pray in faith when you believe that you received (or have) what you pray for when you pray. When praying the prayer of faith you don't wait until you see the answer before you believe you have it. You believe you receive it AT THE TIME that you are praying. The world has a saying "I won't believe it until I see it." Praying with this attitude is not praying in faith.

Q. What is the difference between faith and belief?

A. Confusion and a lack of knowledge in this very crucial area of the Christian walk have caused millions of believers to suffer in poverty and sickness. Believing is having knowledge of something. Faith, on the other hand, is acting on that knowledge. Believing is necessary and good, but it falls far short of faith. For instance, you may believe that if you flip a switch the light will come on. Your faith is not in the switch but the power behind the switch.

Q. In what areas can you exercise faith? What can you believe for?

A. In faith, you can believe for anything the Word of God promises. You cannot, however, believe beyond what the Word promises. Faith is based on what God's Word says.

Q. How do you release your faith?

A. With WORDS. We have been made in the image of God. So, for us to receive the things of God we must do the same thing God does when He wants something—speak. According to the first chapter of Genesis, God began everything with words. "And God said, Let there be light: and there was light." In Mark 11:23 we are instructed to "speak" to our mountains. Everything God created was spoken into existence. Likewise, we must operate by the same principle to receive the same results. Release your faith with WORDS!

Q. What is the "winning formula" for developing faith?

A. Do these things: 1) Find the promises in God's Word for whatever you are seeking, then stand on them; 2) Meditate on God's promises, believing them and speaking them out; 3) Refuse to look at the circumstances; 4) Praise God for the answer as though it had already come; 5) Receive the blessing with thanksgiving; 6) Take "baby steps" and develop your faith with small things before taking on the larger ones.

www.Faith-It-Til-You-Make-It.com

Chapter 3
How to Be a Rich Christian
Jump Start Your Prosperity

Now that you understand the principles of faith, you can get started doing something about yourself and the direction you are headed in life.

Are you tired of living on "Barely Making It Street," just north of the border in "Not Enough, Alabama"? Do you wonder why some people who may not even profess to be Christians seem to be doing so much better financially than you? Have you been tithing, giving love offerings, living right in every way you know how, and yet, blessings always seem to pass you by?

There is a reason all these things seem to be plaguing you. And it's found in the Bible. And there are some steps you can take that will position you for receiving all that God has promised to prosper you-in every area of your life.

Five of those steps are discussed in this chapter. But before we go there, let's take a look at what it means to prosper.

True prosperity involves the entire man—not just money! And only God's Word can lead to true prosperity. If you learn to live, think, speak, give and act right, in accordance with the Word of God, there is nothing or no one who can stop you from prospering. Once you tap into the favor of God you will realize that favor is better then money! You will become empowered to do what God called you to do in the earth because you are not burdened with need, lack and basic things that distract us from our true destiny: evangelism.

Knowledge is the key that separates the poor from

the rich. Everything that exists here on earth has existed in some form or another since the time of Adam and Eve. Computers, cars, skyscrapers, and all modern technology have progressed based on man's research, application of what was learned and his diligent use of materials that were provided by God.

To prosper is defined as "the supernatural ability to meet the needs of mankind, regardless of those needs. Being in control of your circumstances at all times." The word "rich" means "the absence of lack and the presence of choices."

For years, prosperity has been a controversial topic when it comes to the Church. It's all around us.

Almost everywhere we go, we hear something about prosperity. There are books, tapes, and radio and TV talk shows, even financial seminars, all centered on the theme of prospering.

Even non-Christian sponsors are bombarding the infomercial market with "get rich quick" offers. It goes without saying: this nation is clearly focused on increase, or prosperity.

And that begs another question.

With all this wealth of information at our disposal, why is the Church operating in a pitiful state of perpetual lack?

The answer is DEMONIC STRONGHOLDS.

I minister an average of 150 concerts and speaking engagements each year. In each service, I make a point of asking the question, "Who needs money?"

In most of those services, nearly every person will raise his hand. The willingness to take some sort of instruction on how to get money is ever present when the practical idea of having money is mentioned. But something happens when you go from talking about needing money to the subject of prosperity.

People become skeptical, guarded, judgmental, and doubtful. Walls go up. It's as though you're talking heresy or something. It's a much different response than when you mention the message of salvation, deliverance and healing.

Why? Because of Satan, that's why. He knows that, if he can keep the Body of Christ confused concerning finances, he can keep the Church from its mission of spreading of the Gospel.

If he can keep you from knowing your heritage in the New Birth, and God's will that you prosper, he can keep you poor.

But God does not want you poor. He does not want you struggling and living from paycheck to paycheck. He says: "I would that you should prosper and be in health, even as your soul prospers." God cares that you prosper. And He has fixed it so that you can.

But before you can walk in what God has provided for you, you have to know what He has provided. If you don't know you have it, you cannot use it.

"My people perish for lack of knowledge (Hosea 4:6)."

You see, God has established a covenant with man. And He will see to it that that covenant is kept. But for that to happen, He has to work through a man. God will not show up in the flesh to establish His covenant and minister the Word to the nations. He has chosen man to do that for Him.

In order to perform this task, MAN is going to need finances. Those finances will have to come from the Body of Christ. If the Body is broke, busted, and disgusted, then it can't be of much effect in this effort. This isn't rocket science, folks. You simply can't give what you don't have. A broke Christian is no threat to anyone. A Christian without his money is like a policeman without his uniform. He has authority but nobody knows it (or believes it). Satan knows that.

But a Christian who knows his rights in Christ, who knows it is God's will for him to prosper, and will be led by the Spirit of God and His Word, can stop all the forces of the enemy.

In the last several years, God has allowed me to learn many of His truths concerning finances and prosperity. By properly applying these, I have seen my status change from one of poverty to overflowing abundance. I was born into poverty. No one can say that Ben Tankard was born with a silver spoon in his mouth. Our groceries consisted of welfare cheese (very hard), peanut butter (also very hard), powdered eggs (very nasty) and powdered milk (also very nasty). One of my odd jobs was shoveling chicken manure on a chicken farm. As an adult one of my worst jobs was a dogcatcher.

Today, my family lives under God's divine provision. We are totally self contained, meaning when God tells us to do something, we don't have to ask anybody's permission, wait in any long lines or be put on someone else's schedule or timetable. As a result of the blessings of the Lord, we never have a bad day.

My wife, Jewel, and I are the happiest couple on earth. We have never had an argument or so much as a disagreement. We are always happy! Now some people will say that money can't buy happiness. That is certainly true, however money can eliminate the day-to- day struggle of working two and three jobs to make ends meet. Money can make the phone stop ringing from nasty bill collectors. Money can eliminate all the material needs in your life. Money does answer ALL things. Whether or not you become "happy" about all these things is simply a matter of choice. The average person thinks about money (or getting more of it) at least 40 hours a week! Just imagine if that burden was lifted from your shoulders and you could spend that 40 hours a week meditating on the WORD, spreading the message of truth, and getting some unbelievers saved! Most marriages suffer from evil financial arguments. Of course the wife does not feel like any after hours "hanky-panky" with the husband…she has worked three jobs, picked up the kids, cooked, cleaned and finally got them in the bed! She barely has time to think. But if there were no lack, she would not have to work to "help-out." There would be more time to prepare for the man of God (her husband), then Victoria's secret would not have to be a secret anymore.

Most sicknesses are brought on by stress that is induced by lack. Most crimes are birthed from lack. Eliminate lack and you cover 90 percent of your problems and issues.

In the following pages, I will share with you many of the Biblical principles we have used for our success. Properly applied, they will work for you just as they have worked for us. *God is not a respecter of persons (Acts 10:34).* What He does for one, He will do for everyone. But you have a part to play.

If you're seeking a deeper understanding of prosperity—and I'm sure you do, otherwise, you would not have read this far—make a quality decision now. Decide now that you will be open to what the Bible has to say about prosperity.

With an open mind, you position yourself to be ready to receive what God has already established for you. Be ready to change, and you'll see just how quickly you will change.

God is ready to bless and prosper you. But He will need your cooperation.

Negative Mindset

If you are reading this book, more than likely it's because you are in need of more money. That's nothing to be ashamed of because most of us do.

Before we look at what we can do to satisfy that need, let's look at some of the reasons most people find themselves broke, and in financial need. These are some of the mindsets that need to be shed before you can renew your mind and develop a mentality of prosperity.

Some of what you read here may be seem a bit humorous. That's intentional. I'm well aware that poverty is not a funny matter. But neither is condemnation. While we might recognize that the reason we're living in abject poverty is because of things we have done wrong for years, there is no sense in beating ourselves over the head for it.

What's done is done. We cannot change it. But with the proper teaching, we can start over. That's what this book is about-a new beginning.

The Poverty Spirit

Many of you are familiar with comedian Jeff Foxworthy and his comic routine "You Might Be a Redneck If..." Well, consider these statements as we say, "You Might Have a Poverty Spirit If:"

•You think being broke makes you more "spiritual."

•You say things like "All those preachers want is

your money" or "It don't take all that."

•You ask for change for $5 before you give an offering in church.

•You still have plastic on your rent-a-center furniture.

•You have to pray in the spirit while the store clerk calls the bank to approve your check.

•You think the meaning of *"Mutual Fund"* is when you and I are having a good time.

•You re-use plastic spoons, forks and paper plates.

•You think praying for "just enough" is a sign of humility.

•You buy everything on layaway.

•The relatives you consider rich live in a mobile home.

•Your answer machine is on 24/7 to screen bill collectors.

•Your car constantly runs out of gas even though you have money in your pocket.

•You think "super sizing" your favorite fast food meal is a special occasion.

•You have to take a week or more of vacation from work to attend an out-of-town family event because you have to drive.

•You automatically gravitate to the sale racks when shopping.

•You read a restaurant menu from right to left.

•You still use a clothes hanger as a TV antenna.

•You have two TVs in your living room, but there is no picture on one and no sound on the other.

•You make copies of teaching or music tapes instead of buying the tapes.

•You bought new clothes for the Kirk Franklin concert and returned them to the store the next day.

•Your desk has countless unopened bills from the same creditors for the last six months.

•Your idea of a vacation is two weeks of uninterrupted soap operas.

•You think jury duty is a good way to make money.

•You have French fries from last week's McDonald's combo on the floor of your car.

•Your apartment smells like old diapers but you say you'll wait until you get into the "big house" to start cleaning up.

I said some of these would be funny. But the humor doesn't take away from the seriousness of the subject. The more you act out poverty, the deeper you become grounded in it.

Listen, folks. You have got to get rid of these mindsets! They are false. And they are destructive. The common element that is the "glue" for all my teachings is faith. With faith, you can accomplish anything— including becoming a millionaire.

Anything worth having requires work. And I'm here to tell you, if you intend to change your wrong thinking to right thinking, it will take some work. So get ready.

Get ready to turn loose of all the "village losers" in your life, the ones who will speak against the things of God and try to hinder your faith. Get ready to spend more time in God's Word, and to practice living what He commands you to.

I believe you are up to the challenge though. If you are sick and tired of being sick and tired, you're up to the challenge. You have nowhere to go but up. And besides, what do you have to lose?

Don't abort this baby that's about to be given life in you. Let it develop. And when the time is right for it to come forth, it will come forth in power, might, and prosperity.

Only the truth that you know will set you free. Everything you read here is based on God's Word. It will set you free.

You must change your wrong thinking into right thinking. The following five "rights" will help you do just that.

Step 1 - Live Right!

"If ye be willing and obedient,
ye shall eat the good of the land."
Isaiah 1:19

Before you can expect to cash in on any of God's promises, you must first establish right standing, or righteousness with Him. I don't want to take anything for granted. If you are not a born-again Christian, your first step to walking in His divine prosperity is to establish a right relationship with Him. To do that, I encourage you to turn to the back of this book, where you will find the prayer for salvation.

If you are already a believer, then let me encourage you that God has never had a problem with His children having money and prospering. He just wants you to do it HIS way.

As a believer, you must learn to walk in complete honesty and integrity. You cannot lie, cheat, steal, commit adultery or live in habitual sin and expect God to prosper you. Can you believe there are some who are guilty of these things, and will literally get angry with God when their prayers are not answered?

My friend, you may be able to fool man but God sees it all. He knows what you are doing, every time you do it. If you think you are getting away you are mistaken. You are living in denial. You have to call sin what it is-sin. Then deal with it. Get right with God so that He can begin to set things right in your life. Don't get me wrong. I'm not saying that I am some perfect faith giant. No, I'm human just like you. I have to pay for past mistakes and I have to rebuke Satan's attacks continually just like the next person. But like David, I have a heart for God. And I strive continually for excellence in every area of my life.

We all make mistakes. God knows that. That's why He gave us that wonderful scripture in 1 John 1:9, which says: "If we confess our sins, he is faithful and just to forgive us our sins, and cleanse us from all unrighteousness."

God is in the cleansing business. And that includes cleaning you up and forgiving you of all your wrongs. You may fall flat on your face. But God will always be there to pick you up, brush you off and give you a fresh start. You put it all in motion when first: you recognize your wrong; second, confess your wrong; and third, ask God's forgiveness of your wrong. The rest is up to Him.

The scripture says in 2 Corinthians 6:17, *"come out and be ye separated."* In order to **walk** into favor you have to **run** from sin.

Just as our bodies process food without us having to tell our digestive systems to do so, just as we breathe without telling our lungs to inhale and exhale, so the system of God's Kingdom, which includes prosperity, operates without any assistance from us.

When we operate by His system of obedience, trusting in His Word and doing what He instructs us to do, then the supernatural blessings of God will begin to flow. As soon as you begin to put God first, you begin to see some changes.

Starting today, you will begin to walk in favor and prosperity, health and wealth in God. And it will result in a sweatless success! As you learn how to live your life according to the Word of God, you will become a money magnet.

Begin by seeking God daily. Get into His presence by spending time in prayer and His Word. This will position you to receive what God has promised you as His "heir".

Money is looking for you!

Step 2 - Think Right!

"For as he thinketh in his heart, so is he."
Proverbs 23:7

I once heard someone say, "Those who expect little are never disappointed." This is very true. The scriptures back it up, as you can see in the above verse from Proverbs. Whatever a man thinks will be manifested in his lifestyle. If he thinks small, he will get small. If he thinks big, he will get big. You need to "baptize" your thoughts in a higher realm. If it is not on your mind it is not in your future!

Another scripture that supports this thinking is found in Galatians 6:7.

"For whatsoever a man soweth, that shall he also reap."

You are going to have to make a quality decision to change the way you think about yourself, and about your situation. One thing you must settle from the beginning and that is God is good, and the devil is bad. Bad things do not come from God. If you're in bad shape financially, it's not God's fault. So, don't blame it on Him. Put the blame where it belongs.

"But the thief (Satan) cometh not, but for the steal, and to kill and to destroy. I (Jesus) come that they might have life, and that they may have it more abundantly."

You see. It is not God who causes bad things to happen in your life. It is the devil. He is the thief, the robber, and the murderer. But in some cases we can't blame the devil for our own bad decisions. There are spiritual, physical and natural laws that, once set in motion, will naturally work on their own. For instance, if you dropped a glass of grape juice on a white carpet that carpet is going to stain. There are no two ways about it. It's a law of gravity and you cannot blame gravity, God or the devil.

The fact is YOU dropped the juice.

You can't say it was the devil trying to steal your voice because you messed up during your solo last Sunday morning in church. Not if you spent all Saturday night smoking cigarettes.

Since childhood, we were taught to recite the 23rd Psalm. But not very many of us took the time to meditate those words to understand exactly what they were saying to us.

This is a Psalm of blessing and praise. It honors God as our Shepherd, Provider, and Keeper.

I like the verse that says "...thou preparest a table before me, in the *presence of mine enemies*". Have you ever considered the fact that we will not have any enemies in Heaven? That means He does this right here, right now, on earth.

Man, that's powerful. God said that in the midst of all my enemies trying to do me harm, He takes time to fix me a full-course meal so that I can be nourished. What an awesome God we serve.

When you begin to understand what God has in store for you, you can begin to change your thinking process. You start to think rich instead of poor. You think above instead of beneath. You think like you're the head and not the tail. (Deut. 28:13.).

In your spirit, you see yourself soaring with the eagles instead of nesting with the chickens

A Mind Change
So, how does this happen?

It begins when the Word of God renews your mind.

In Romans 12:2, we read: *"And be ye transformed by the renewing of your mind..."*

The world's system dictates that you have to work two jobs to make ends meet, or to get ahead. The world's system says you can only have one week of vacation per year, and will have to work until you are 65 before you can retire. Even then, what you get in Social Security won't be enough to meet all of your needs.

Do you think this is what Jesus would be doing if He were still here on earth? Of course not. Jesus is King of Kings, and Lord of Lords. He owns it all. And you know what? As joint heirs with Him, we have everything He has.

So, why don't we act like it? Why do we accept a life sentence of endless work and little pay with long hours and hardly any time to spend with our families? Why do we never have enough money to do what we would like to do, let alone what God has called us to do regarding financing the end time harvest of souls into the Kingdom?

Why do we punish ourselves?

We must put an end to what I call "stinking thinking".

How? There are three ways.

First, we must decide that we will not be defeated and that we will receive from God. (1 John 5:4-5)

Second, resist Satan and his attacks on your mind and stop entertaining his thoughts. (2 Corinthians 10:3-5)

Third, you must develop the habit of studying the Word daily. The psalmist, David, said "Thy word have I hid in my heart that I might not sin against thee."

"This book of the law shall not depart out of thy mouth; but thou shalt meditate therein day and night that thou mayest observe to do according to all that is written therein: for then thou shalt make thy way prosperous, and then thou shalt have good success (Joshua 1:8)."

"Blessed is the man that walketh not in the counsel of the ungodly, nor standeth in the way of sinners, nor sitteth in the seat of the scornful. But his delight is in the law of the Lord and in his law doth he meditate day and night. And he shall be like a tree planted by the rivers of water, that bringeth forth his fruit in his season; his leaf also shall not wither; and whatsoever he doeth shall prosper (Psalms 1:1-3)."

Notice what it says you get in return for meditating on the Word day and night. You get "good success" and "whatsoever you do prospers"! Sounds like a good deal to me.

There's a saying that goes something like "Whatever you do for 21 days straight will become a habit." You should try it. Find scriptures that deal with increase, prosperity and finance and study them for 21 days. Be sure and apply what you're studying to your own situation during that time. Then, see what happens. I can tell you what will happen. You'll see a major turnaround in your life, your finances and your prosperity.

God's Word is sure. It won't fail.

You'll find yourself wanting to know more and more and more about those subjects. It will become just as important to you as eating food for the nourishment of your body. In fact, you are feeding your body-and your spirit.

To become rich on the outside you must first become rich on the inside. Become a goal-setter. Get a vision of what you want or where you desire to be a year from now, two years from now. Whatever. Set aside time to dream about the things you want. Then, see what the Word has to say about them.

No, I don't mean you can dream about a Lexus or a BMW and find the promise for that dream somewhere in the Bible. Don't be ridiculous. What I'm saying is that God will show you how to apply your faith towards getting whatever it is you want. Just make sure your desires are in line with God's Word.

We're told in scripture to write the vision on the wall, to keep it before us. What you feed your spirit man governs your thought life. If you study and meditate on good things, then you'll always be thinking on those things. They become your life, your vision. And soon enough, they will become reality in your life.

Here are some things you can do to stir your faith.

If you want a new house, start reading magazines about homes. Cut out pictures of the house you like and put them on your refrigerator door. Order blueprints and house plans and study them. You can do the same thing for cars, businesses and properties. Create a "vision board" or "wall of faith" in your home.

Begin to see yourself owning that house, that car or that piece of property. Start planting seeds for the things you want. See yourself sowing large seeds into other ministries, then start sowing whatever you can.

As I mentioned in chapter one, take out an old checkbook and practice writing checks for $1,000, $5,000, $10,000 or more to a ministry of your choosing, to family and friends. (Just remember, this is practice. Don't give those checks out if you don't have that kind of money in the bank).

Don't be like some people who write what they call "faith checks," knowing they don't have the money to cover them but believing that God will do a miracle and somehow make the money appear in the bank before the check gets there.

God won't honor that kind of "faith." Besides, it is unlawful to write checks knowing you don't have the funds in the bank to cover them. Oh yes, He is faithful and He will be with you-all the way to the county jail.

Stick with practicing for now. Soon, it will be a reality in your life.

Remember the soldiers who were afraid to go out and fight Goliath? They thought he was too big to hit. Well, the little shepherd boy, David, had a different thought. He looked at that oversized Philistine and thought he was *too big to MISS*. His victory was founded on a winning thought life.

Meditating God's Word will help you to change your thinking. You'll begin to see what you thought were impossibilities as possibilities.

When I walk into a room, I stand tall and look around as if I can BUY the whole building. You will find that people treat you the way you think of yourself. If you think you are poor, people will treat you like you are always looking for a handout.

In playing college and professional basketball one of the things our team noticed was the way we thought of ourselves often determined the outcome of our ballgames. Even if we thought we would sometimes be outsized, we still got off the bus or plane like we were undefeated!

The Israelites followed Moses out of Egyptian bondage, but then they failed to enter into the Promised Land because they feared the "giant" occupants. They had a "grasshopper mentality."

"We be not able to defeat them...we were in our own sight as grasshoppers, and so we were in their sight..." *(Numbers 13:30-33).*

The giants never even touched them. It was their small thinking that became their downfall.

Stay away from the "we be nots" of the world. Get into the Word and begin to develop a dream of winning. Begin thinking right. How long will you wait before you possess what God intended for you?

*"And Joshua said unto the children of Israel, How long are ye **slack** to go to possess the land, which the LORD God of your fathers hath given you (Josh.18:3)?"*

Here are some scriptures that will remind you of your covenant, help you renew your mind and prove to you that you are supposed to be fat (rich and wealthy)!

Fat

Psalms 22:29: All they that be **fat** upon earth shall eat and worship.

Psalms 92:14: They shall still bring forth fruit in old age; they shall be **fat** and flourishing.

Proverbs 11:25: The liberal soul shall be made **fat**: and he that watereth shall be watered also himself.

Proverbs 13:4: The soul of the sluggard desireth, and

hath nothing: but the soul of the diligent shall be made **fat**.

Proverbs 28:25: He that is of a proud heart stirreth up strife: but he that putteth his trust in the LORD shall be made **fat.**

Rich

2 Corinthians 8:9: For ye know the grace of our Lord Jesus Christ, that, though he was **rich**, yet for your sakes he became poor, that ye through his poverty might be **rich** .

1Timothy 6:17... God, who giveth us **richly** all things to enjoy;

Proverbs 10:4: He becometh poor that dealeth with a slack hand: but the hand of the diligent maketh **rich.**

Genesis 13:2: And Abram was very **rich** in cattle, in silver, and in gold.

Proverbs 10:15: The **rich** man's wealth is his strong city: the destruction of the poor is their poverty.

Proverbs 10:22: The blessing of the LORD, it maketh **rich** and he addeth no sorrow with it.

Proverbs 14:20: The poor is hated even of his own neighbour: but the **rich** hath many friends.

Proverbs 22:7: The **rich** ruleth over the poor, and the

borrower is servant to the lender.

Increase

1Thessalonians 4:10: And indeed ye do it toward all the brethren which are in all Macedonia: but we beseech you, brethren, that ye **increase** more and more.

Deuteronomy 6:3: Hear therefore, O Israel, and observe to do it; that it may be well with thee, and that ye may **increase** mightily, as the LORD God of thy fathers hath promised thee, in the land that floweth with milk and honey.

Deuteronomy 32:13: He made him ride on the high places of the earth, that he might eat the **increase** of the fields; and he made him to suck honey out of the rock, and oil out of the flinty rock.

Job 8:7: Though thy beginning was small, yet thy latter end should greatly **increase.**
Psalms 115:14: The LORD shall **increase** you more and more, you and your children.

Prosper

3 John 1:2: Beloved, I wish above all things that thou mayest **prosper** and be in health, even as thy soul prospereth.

Genesis 39:23: The keeper of the prison looked not to any thing that was under his hand; because the LORD was with him, and that which he did, the LORD made it to **prosper**.

1Kings 2:3: And keep the charge of the LORD thy God, to walk in his ways, to keep his statutes, and his commandments, and his judgments, and his testimonies, as it is written in the law of Moses, that thou mayest **prosper** in all that thou doest, and whithersoever thou turnest thyself:

2 Chronicles 20:20: Believe his prophets, so shall ye **prosper**.

2 Chronicles 26:5: ... and as long as he sought the LORD, God made him to **prosper.**

Psalms 1:3: And he shall be like a tree planted by the rivers of water, that bringeth forth his fruit in his season; his leaf also shall not wither; and whatsoever he doeth shall **prosper**.

Prosperity

Job 36:11: If they obey and serve him, they shall spend their days in **prosperity**, and their years in pleasures.

Psalms 35:27: Let them shout for joy, and be glad, that favour my righteous cause: yea, let them say continually, Let the LORD be magnified, which hath pleasure in the **prosperity** of his servant.

Psalms 118:25: Save now, I beseech thee, O LORD: O LORD, I beseech thee, send now **prosperity**.

Psalms 122:7: Peace be within thy walls, and **prosperity** within thy palaces.

Wealth

Psalms 66:12: Thou hast caused men to ride over our heads; we went through fire and through water: but thou broughtest us out into a **wealthy** place.

Deuteronomy 8:18: But thou shalt remember the LORD thy God: for it is he that giveth thee power to get **wealth**, that he may establish his covenant which he sware unto thy fathers, as it is this day.

Proverbs 10:15: The rich man's **wealth** is his strong city: the destruction of the poor is their poverty.

Proverbs 13:22: A good man leaveth an inheritance to his children's children: and the **wealth** of the sinner is laid up for the just.

Money

Proverbs 7:20: He hath taken a bag of **money** with him, and will come home at the day appointed.

Ecclesiastes 7:12: For wisdom is a defence, and **money** is a defence.

Ecclesiastes 10:19: A feast is made for laughter, and wine maketh merry: but **money answereth all things!!**

Step 3 - Speak Right!

*Thou shalt also decree a thing
and it shall be established.*
Job 22:28

Christianity is sometimes referred to as *the great confession*. But did you know that most Christians are defeated because they believe and confess the wrong things. *"Thou art snared with the words of thy mouth."* *(Proverbs 6:1-2)*

Words are the most powerful things in the universe! Words spoken in faith can make you rich, but words spoken out of fear can bring destruction. I like what Brother Kenneth Copeland says: "Faith is to God what fear is to the devil."

God used faith in His own words to create the universe. The Bible says that it was by faith that the world was framed. It's the same faith, the God kind of faith, that we must use to see things come to past in our life.

Listen friend, faith and fear cannot co-exist. Something has to give. Either you exercise your faith in God to see the natural become the supernatural, or you let fear take over and go with what the devil is telling you.

Rather than choose sides with the devil and wallow in defeat, make a decision to release your faith in God's Word over whatever the situation is and see God go to work for you.

What makes you the architect of your own future? Your WORDS-that's what! Begin to speak your dreams out loud. The more you hear yourself say something, the more you will believe it. Remember, faith cometh by hearing, and hearing, and hearing.

Spiritual Law

It is a spiritual law that, as born-again believers, we have been made in the image of God. So, in order to obtain the things of God, we must do the same things God does when He wants something-speak! God never does anything without first saying it. God is a faith God. He releases His faith through His words.

As pointed out earlier, we are instructed in Mark 11:23 to "speak" to our mountains.

Read Genesis 1 and notice how many times the words "God said" occur. Every time He created something, God spoke it first.

To get the same results, we must operate in the same manner and by the same principle. Release your faith with WORDS! Refuse to speak words that are contrary to what you believe you have received.

Deal With Doubt, Immediately!

As soon as doubt rears its ugly head, deal with it-immediately! And use the Word. If it's a matter concerning sickness, find scripture that states God position on sickness and use it to combat that doubt.

If you're dealing with a financial situation, remember what God's Words said about your needs. "My God shall supply all of my needs according to his riches in glory by Christ Jesus." Declare war on debt and lack with your words.

Say out loud: "I'm rich. I have more than enough and I am able to bless others without measure."

Say it 500 times a day if you have to. But say it until it gets down inside you. Until you hear it, believe it, and stand on it. Don't give the enemy even the slightest foothold by allowing doubts and fears to enter in. Answer every doubt immediately with the Word of God. Answer every symptom of poverty and lack immediately with the Word of God. Let all of your answers be based on the Word.

Next, make the decision that you will never complain or speak evil against another person again. I know this can be very challenging. Especially considering how some people act. But complaining, as God says in the book of Numbers, is sin. And so is speaking against others. Remember, God is your source. He meets your needs. He also blesses those whose hearts are fixed on Him, and not the cares of this world.

If you want something to replace your conversation of complaining, I suggest you look at the "Increase Scriptures" listed in this book again. Begin to confess them daily, inserting your name to make it personal. You will soon find yourself meditating God's Word and not even thinking about those around you and what they do to you.

Words are containers. They carry faith or fear, and they produce after their own kind. Since God does not lie, the safest way to operate is to confess what He says. Say what He says about your situation and what it could work out to your good.

The doctor or bank officer may have a bad report, but the Word always promises the good report-despite your circumstances. Begin to confess victory in the face of defeat. Speak abundance in the face of lack. Think about it. You have nothing to lose and everything to gain. If you had everything you needed you would not be reading this book. In fact, if your current system was working that well you would probably be writing your own book.

Your heart, and your situation will change as you believe and receive the Word. Speak the answer, not the problem. Stop saying what you have and start having what God says. If you want to be a rich Christian, you are going to have to begin to speak right.

Don't be afraid to *speak those things that be not as though they were.* In fact, your confessions for future prayers should sound just like your confessions for past blessings. I remember when I started making the positive confession that I was a "million-heir." Some gospel music magazines interviewed me and ran articles about my new "million-heir" mentality and message. Well, the devil got mad at my bold statement of faith and began to attack me.

I was subpoenaed to a child-support deposition and, with the intent to "trap" me with my own words, the attorney asked me if it were true that I said I was a "million-heir" in these magazines? I said, "yes I said that but those articles were old. Now I'm a billion-heir!"

You see, when you start confessing God's Word and going against that old broke Christian, doom-and-gloom-and-struggle religion, not everybody is going to be happy.

Step 4 - Give Right!

Whatever a man sows, that will he also reap.
Gal. 6:7

This step has been a stumbling block for many
Believers because, when it comes to giving out of
obedience, the flesh always wants to get in the way. Let
me ask you something. Did you receive any money
from IBM last year? What about McDonald's or Burger
King? If your answer is "no", then it is probably
because none of those companies owed you anything.
So, why should they have given you something?

Well, the Lord says that's why He has not blessed
some of us. He does not owe us anything. You see there
are two sides of the covenant we have with the Mighty
God. There is the God-ward (or blessing) side, and the
Man-ward (obedience) side. You access the God-ward
side of the covenant by first performing the Man-ward
side.

Here are some acts of obedience that you must
perform to receive the blessings of God and experience
true wealth.

Give to the Poor

Be honest. When was the last time you gave to the
poor?

The Bible says *"He that hath pity upon the poor
lendeth unto the Lord: and that which he hath given will
he pay him again (Proverbs 9:17)..."* Can you imagine
how good it must feel to stand before God knowing that
He owes you-not because He's indebted to you, but
because of your obedience?

Most Christians do not understand how important it

is to give-especially to the poor.

Pay Your Tithe!

"Bring ye all the tithes into the storehouse, that there may be meat in mine house, and prove me now herewith, saith the Lord of hosts, if I will not open you the windows of heaven, and pour you out a blessing, that there shall not be room enough to receive it. And I will rebuke the devourer for your sakes, and he shall not destroy the fruits of your ground; neither shall your vine cast her fruit before the time in the field."(Malachi 3:10-11).

It's a command, not an option.

This is God Himself speaking, and He is saying "bring your tithe into My storehouse." But notice what He says after giving such a strong directive.

"Prove Me," God says.

This is the only place in the Bible where God tells us to do something, and then instructs us to prove Him-put Him to the test to see if He will do what He says. It is also the one place where most people have pulled back and have not taken advantage of seeing God work on their behalf.

Not only is tithing an act of obedience, it is an honor.

"Honour the Lord with thy substance, and with the first fruits of all thine increase." (Proverbs 3:9)

Tithing puts God in the position of rebuking the devourer (Satan) on your behalf (Malachi 3:11). In a nutshell, the tithe is your "Spiritual Protection Money".

When you give 10 percent of your earnings to God, God protects the remaining 90 percent from the forces of hell. If you don't tithe-look out! You've just given Satan an open door to wreak havoc on your finances because you've removed yourself from God's covenant protection.

It's like an insurance policy. Fail to pay the premium, and you are still covered for what is referred to as a "grace" period. But sooner of later, grace runs out and you're open prey to whatever happens. When you tithe, you are under the protection of an open Heaven. Stop tithing and you close the door and windows of Heaven, and the protection is not available to you.

The Bible says that the wealth of the wicked is laid up for the just. That's us, my friend. We have been made righteous, or just by the Blood of Jesus Christ. It is God who gives us the power to get wealth.

If we are operating in obedience to God's Word, then we can expect to receive His blessings. If we are not walking in obedience, we are considered part of the wicked club and our wealth is being laid up for some other JUST person.

Tithing the Tithe!

A general rule of thumb when paying tithes is to separate your tithe from the rest of your income immediately-before you begin spending the remaining 90 percent. By doing this, the tithe truly becomes your "first fruit." If you wait until Sunday to give your tithe, and you have already spent the rest of your check, then what you give God is not truly your "first fruit." It is your last fruit.

You must learn to be more diligent with God's money than you are with your money.

For instance, if you needed to pay an electric bill, phone bill or some other bill, and you had a cutoff notice facing you, you would find a way to make that payment on time.

You should take that same approach where God's tithe is concerned. Why wait until Sunday, when you go to church, to give God what belongs to Him. The quicker you pay your tithe (the premium), the quicker your coverage starts!

Another matter regarding the tithe that gets people into financial bondage concerns the question of whether to pay tithe on the gross or the net.

I believe that the attitude of the heart is what should shine through. God does not need your money. He desires your obedience. If you work for someone other than yourself, there are a couple of ways to look at tithe. The safest way is to pay tithe on whatever your salary is (gross) because you can never give God too much.

Many people have certain deductions taken out of their salary before they receive it. These include such things as car loans, insurance, savings and taxes. In addition, by the time they get their check, half of their bills have already been paid directly through bank draft.

If you tithe only on what you receive in your check after all of these deductions have occurred, you are not really tithing on your total income. And you're cheating God.

One of the benefits (not that we're after the benefits, here) is that when you tithe on the gross you are also tithing on whatever taxes that come out of your paycheck. That means you have already tithed on that income tax check you will receive at tax time.

Now, if you are self-employed then you have to consider what true "increase" is. You pay tithe on your increase, not your income. For instance, if you sell cars you may purchase a car wholesale for $3,000. You may then sell that same care for $5,000. Your income on the sale is $5,000, but your actual increase or profit is only

$2,000. I believe you should pay tithe on the $2,000.

While some might argue that you should tithe on the entire $5,000, I don't believe you should get into bondage over it. As I said earlier, you never can give God too much.

To Whom Should You Tithe?

Where you place your tithe depends on where you are receiving your spiritual food and leadership. The Bible says to bring all the tithes into the storehouse (Malachi 3:10). The storehouse is the place where you are being fed, and nurtured spiritually.

When you pay your tithe, you are not giving it to an individual. You are giving it for the furtherance of the gospel. Because the tithe belongs to God, and since Jesus is the One Who receives and actually presents it to God, you should always pray and let Him tell you where it should be put to work.

Finally, tithing consists of two parts. First, there's the giving or presenting of the tithe, which is done in gratitude and worship. Second, is the receiving from Him for your obedience.

There is a great blessing in tithing. As we said earlier, it is the one area where God gives us clear-cut instructions, then tells us to put Him to the test in terms of how He will respond to our obedience.

Recognize the importance of the tithe. When you do, it becomes something more than just a symbolic ritual. When you present your tithe, don't just mail it or drop it in a bucket in a haphazard fashion. There is worship involved in the tithe. There is praise involved in the tithe.

Here is a confession you can consider using whenever you present your tithe to God. If you wish, you can establish a confession of your own.

Tithe Confession

I confess this day to You, Lord God, that I have come into the inheritance which You swore to give me. I am in the land that You have provided for me in Jesus Christ, the kingdom of Almighty God. I was a sinner serving Satan. He was my god. But I called upon the Name of Jesus and You heard my cry and delivered me from the power and authority of darkness and translated me into the kingdom of Your dear Son. Jesus, as my Lord and High Priest, I bring the first fruits of my increase to You and worship God with it. I have hearkened to the voice of the Lord my God and have done according to all that You have commanded me. Now, I believe You will look down from Your holy habitation in heaven and bless me as You said in Your Word. I confess that the windows of heaven are being opened. Blessings are being poured out, and there is not enough room to receive them! Surely I will shout, "It is enough! It is enough!"

Give a DAILY Offering: (this includes missions and blessing your Pastor or spiritual father as well as miscellaneous offerings)

Now, here is a tip that will bring even greater blessings to you. Learn to give on a daily basis.

The Word tells us that we will reap what we sow. This is very true where finances are concerned. The fact is you get a harvest on whatever you plant. If you plant watermelon seeds, I don't care how long and how hard you pray, you will not reap a crop of eggplant. You're going to get watermelons. Put squash seeds in the ground, and you'll reap a harvest of squash.

It's the same with money. If you have a need for money, then you're going to have to plant money. It's the process of sowing and reaping.

The frequency with which you sow money will determine how often you reap money. For instance, if you own a business and need money coming in every day then you should be giving or sowing into somebody else's ministry every day.

In addition, the amount of money you sow determines how much you receive. You have the right to claim a hundred-fold return on whatever you sow. That's biblical. If your gift does not move you, it doesn't move God!

"But he shall receive an hundredfold now in this time, houses, and brethren, and sisters, and mothers, and children, and lands, with persecutions; and in the world to come eternal life " (Mark 10:30).

There is one particular ministry that I send an offering to every day. Not every other day. Not every week or so, but every single day-including Sunday. And I am doing it joyfully.

That's biblical, too.

Sometimes my offering may be as much as $1,000. Sometimes it may only be $1. That's not the point. The key is that I send in an offering daily. God has entrusted me with a very large, and prosperous ministry. And it takes finances to do all that He has given us to do. I need finances coming in on a daily basis. So, I give on a daily basis.

And trust me, folks, I am seeing the hand of God work in this ministry like never before. Needs are being met. Doors are being opened. We are truly being blessed.

It can and will happen for you, too. Just think, everything in the universe is based on giving and receiving, seedtime and harvest. You can take a breath but you have exhale before you can inhale again. Some of our bank accounts need to exhale before they can inhale. Some of our garages, closets, and attics need to do the same thing. You have to give to get!

One other thing. Once you plant your seed, you should water it with praise and worship and thanksgiving for the harvest. Don't be like a lazy farmer who plants the seed, covers it with soil and walks off, expecting the morning dew to do the watering. No, your seed has to be nourished if it is expected to grow. You have to water it.

If the seed is not watered, it will die.

How do you water your seed? With the Word of God. It's a sorry farmer that will plant a seed and walk away from it, never once watering it or returning to check on it.

That seed will die right where the farmer left it. IT WILL DIE!

Some people, because of their traditional mindsets, condemn Christians who give with the expectation of receiving something in return. This is what I refer to as "stinking-thinking." How can anyone continue to give unless they receive? Besides, the Word of God backs it up.

"Give and it shall be given to you, good measure pressed down, shaken together shall men give unto your bosoms."

Just as God expects you to be consistent in your giving, He will see that you receive on a consistent basis. If you are faithful and diligent in your giving, then you have a right to expect to receive - BIG TIME!

It is important that you realize you are living to give (Ephesians 4:28). Learn to live on the increase from your giving. That is, reach for the place in your financial life where the income from your job or business becomes your seed for giving.

Heavenly Accounting
"...But he shall receive an hundredfold now in this time..."

Mark 10:30

Did you know you have a financial account in heaven? Well, you do. And every time you plant a seed (above the tithe, which is required) your gift is multiplied by 30, 60 or 100 "fold" (based on your faith) and placed in your "Heavenly account". For example, if you give $1 to the poor or a ministry, Heaven records a deposit of $100 in your account. And that $100 is sitting there just waiting for you to make a withdrawal. When you need it, it's there for the taking. Why? Because you put it there when you sowed that seed-when you gave that gift. God honored your faithfulness by increasing, or multiplying what you gave.

"...lay up for yourselves treasures in heaven, where neither moth nor rust doth corrupt, and where thieves do not break in and steal..."

Matt. 6:20

Once you tap into heaven's economics and God's way of doing things, you will discover you never have to be broke again! MONEY COMETH! This is the best exchange rate around.

Just think, if you gave $1,000 you would have

$100,000 coming back (by faith)! One key to obtaining your return is to EXPECT it, and know how much you have in your account at all times. Keep a record of your giving. Then, when you go before God to request a withdrawal from your "Heavenly account" you should remind God of His promises and your giving.

You know how much money you have in your earthly accounts, right? Then why would you not want to keep up with what is stored up in your "Heavenly account"? Many Christians don't even know they have one, let alone what's in it! No wonder your "heavenly checks" (your prayers) come back marked "Non-Sufficient Funds" or "Account Closed."

If you have not been diligent in this area, now is a great time to start! And as you sow, believe for a hundred-fold harvest. You will be a blessing to others, and out of debt in no time. God will bless you and *"make all grace abound toward you; that ye, always having all sufficiency in all things, may abound to every good work" (2 Corinthians 9:8).*

Learn to be a complete farmer and purge the entire harvest. Be sure and get ALL God has for you. If God sends you $1 million in a burlap bag, tied to the foot of a cow, you should get the money out the bag, milk the cow and then have it butchered and freeze the steaks for later! Hallelujah!

Get the whole hundred-fold harvest! ! Write those faith checks (with your faith filled words) and sign them: *In Jesus Name!!*

Lord Jesus, I plant this seed into _____ (ministry or church) and I believe in its return because You said it. I dedicate it to Your service, to Your affairs, in Jesus' Name. It will be as the loaves and fishes when You used the hundred-fold principle to feed the people. Amen!

In Jesus' Name, I receive now by faith the hundred-fold return on this seed that is in my hand. I do this in obedience to the Word. Satan, in the Name of Jesus, I rebuke you. You are the persecutor. Take your hands off my money! This is not your seed. It is not your land. It belongs to me, and God. Stay out of my garden! Stay off my farm, for the harvest is mine!

Seek God and be led by the spirit in your giving, especially during special "offering appeals". Don't be moved by your emotions, or out of "necessity," but be led by your spirit and your willingness to support the spreading of the Gospel. Always give with the expectation of receiving a return. This way you can continue to help establish the Covenant (It is a false humility to say you are giving and don't expect anything in return...quit lying to yourself and other people!).

Just to get you started, I would suggest that you use the following formula in your giving. 10 percent tithe; 10 to 20 percent special offerings and love gifts (daily giving); 5 percent to the poor.

As I said earlier, be led by the Spirit and know that if you give in faith and follow His leading, you will always have more then enough. You cannot beat God giving. So, give right!

Step 5 - Act Right!

OK, you are now living, thinking, speaking and giving right. The final step is to *act* on your knowledge of the Word. You must do this to begin to see results.

"Therefore whosoever heareth these sayings of mine, and doeth them, I will liken him unto a wise man, which built his house upon a rock: And the rain descended, and the floods came, and the winds blew, and beat upon that house; and it fell not: for it was founded upon a rock.

And every one that heareth these sayings of mine, and doeth them not, shall be likened unto a foolish man, which built his house upon the sand: And the rain descended, and the floods came, and the winds blew, and beat upon that house; and it fell: and great was the fall of it" (Matthew 7:24-27).

Notice how both men heard the Word, and both houses experienced the storm. But the results were completely different.

Acting on the Word placed a foundation under the wise man's house that could not be moved, and his house suffered no loss. The foolish man, on the other hand, had heard the Word but did not do it. He had no foundation when the floods came. His house may have been easier to build, but it had no power to stand. You must do the Word in order to receive the promises of the Word.

"Be ye doers of the Word and not hearers only " (James 1:22).

You must begin to act like you believed you received when you prayed. If you have asked God for finances to pay off some bills, you should have the checks written out, inside a stamped envelope and ready to be mailed. If you are extending your faith for a new car, then you should already have that car already picked out, the insurance priced, and know what accessories you want to put in it. This is known as acting on what you believe and what God's Word says. Faith without works (action) is dead.

You have to listen to the Holy Spirit when you are acting out the blessings. Don't just do what someone else does. When I was believing God for an airplane, God instructed me to start taking flying lessons so I could have a working knowledge of private aviation. The more I hung around the airports the more I received faith to get my airplane! Praise God. Sometimes you may need to just hang around people who have your answer (not your problem). Start hanging around the blessings so you can get a picture of it in your spirit. It will come to past if you are patient.

God always fulfills His end of the Covenant. It is up to YOU to fulfill your end. Prosperity and good success are yours through God's Word. *If ye abide in me, and my words abide in you, ye shall ask what ye will, and it shall be done unto you " (John 15:7).*

Wrap Up!

There you have your five steps to financial abundance. I pray that your minds will be opened, and your hearts turned toward godly increase. Now, go forth and conquer, fellow millionaires! Be sure and write me with your testimonies of victory. By faith, I declare and confess that you have just learned *How To Be A Rich Christian*!

Additional Increase Promises to Live By

Disclaimer: For best results, confess theses scriptures at least five times a day, seven days a week. There is no microwave financial plan available. If you are too lazy to take time to confess and verbalize the Word, then you are too lazy to reap the harvest. It is totally up to you. Insert your name into the scriptures and make it apply directly to you and your family. Example: "The LORD is my (your name) shepherd; I (your name) shall not want." Psalms 23:1

"Bring ye all the tithes into the storehouse, that there may be meat in mine house, and prove me now herewith, saith the LORD of hosts, if I will not open you the windows of heaven, and pour you out a blessing, that there shall not be room enough to receive it. And I will rebuke the devourer for your sakes, and he shall not destroy the fruits of your ground; neither shall your vine cast her fruit before the time in the field, saith the LORD of hosts. And all nations shall call you blessed: for ye shall be a delightsome land, saith the LORD of hosts." **Malachi 3:10-12**

"Beloved, I wish above all things that thou mayest prosper and be in health, even as thy soul prospereth." **3 John 1:2**

"But my God shall supply all your need according to his riches in glory by Christ Jesus." **Philippians 4:19**

"But this I say, He which soweth sparingly shall reap also sparingly; and he which soweth bountifully shall reap also bountifully. Every man according as he purposeth in his heart, so let him give; not grudgingly, or of necessity: for God loveth a cheerful giver. And God is able to make all grace abound toward you; that ye, always having all sufficiency in all things, may abound to every good work." **2 Corinthians 9:6-8**

"I have been young, and now am old; yet have I not seen the righteous forsaken, nor his seed begging bread." **Psalms 37:25**

"The young lions do lack, and suffer hunger: but they that seek the LORD shall not want any good thing." **Psalms. 34:10**

"And all these blessings shall come on thee, and overtake thee, if thou shalt hearken unto the voice of the LORD thy God. Blessed shalt thou be in the city, and blessed shalt thou be in the field. Blessed shall be the fruit of thy body, and the fruit of thy ground, and the fruit of thy cattle, the increase of thy kine, and the flocks of thy sheep. Blessed shall be thy basket and thy store. Blessed shalt thou be when thou comest in, and blessed shalt thou be when thou goest out. The LORD shall cause thine enemies that rise up against thee to be smitten before thy face: they shall come out against thee one way, and flee before thee seven ways. The LORD shall command the blessing upon thee in thy storehouses, and in all that thou settest thine hand unto; and he shall bless thee in the land which the LORD thy God giveth thee." **Deuteronomy 28:2-8**

"And the LORD shall make thee plenteous in goods, in the fruit of thy body, and in the fruit of thy cattle, and in the fruit of thy ground, in the land which the LORD sware unto thy fathers to give thee. The LORD shall open unto thee his good treasure, the heaven to give the rain unto thy land in his season, and to bless all the work of thine hand: and thou shalt lend unto many nations, and thou shalt not borrow. And the LORD shall make thee the head, and not the tail; and thou shalt be above only, and thou shalt not be beneath; if that thou hearken unto the commandments of the LORD thy God, which I command thee this day, to observe and to do them:" **Deuteronomy 28:11-13**

"Give, and it shall be given unto you; good measure, pressed down, and shaken together, and running over, shall men give into your bosom. For with the same measure that ye mete withal it shall be measured to you again." **Luke 6:38**

"Upon the first day of the week let every one of you lay by him in store, as God hath prospered him, that there be no gatherings when I come." **1 Corinthians 16:2**

"And every one that hath forsaken houses, or brethren, or sisters, or father, or mother, or wife, or children, or lands, for my name's sake, shall receive an hundredfold, and shall inherit everlasting life." **Matthew 19:29**

"For God giveth to a man that is good in his sight wisdom, and knowledge, and joy: but to the sinner he giveth travail, to gather and to heap up, that he may give to him that is good before God. This also is vanity and vexation of spirit." **Ecclesiastes 2:26**

"But thou shalt remember the LORD thy God: for it is he that giveth thee power to get wealth, that he may establish his covenant which he sware unto thy fathers, as it is this day." **Deuteronomy 8:18**

"Therefore take no thought, saying, What shall we eat? or, What shall we drink? or, Wherewithal shall we be clothed? (For after all these things do the Gentiles seek:) for your heavenly Father knoweth that ye have need of all these things. But seek ye first the kingdom of God, and his righteousness; and all these things shall be added unto you." **Matthew 6:31-33**

Chapter 4
Every Prayer Answered
No More Bad Days

As we have already pointed out, prayer is the key to a prosperous, fulfilled, and anointed spiritual walk. However, many believers are living beneath their privileges because they are not praying according to the Word of God. They are not achieving positive results in their lives because they are not following the "rules" of prayer.

It's like trying to play baseball under the rules that govern basketball. You may have a little fun, but nobody wins. You will also find it very difficult to maneuver.

This chapter reveals some simple, easy-to-understand Bible-based principles that will teach you how to pray according to the spiritual laws that have been set forth by God. Walking in obedience to God's Word will guarantee 100 percent results to your prayers.

Your Prayer Success

Have you ever been told that God answers prayer with one of three responses—"Yes," "No," or "Not now"? Much of the confusion concerning answered prayer derives from lack of knowledge of God's Word. People tend to blame things on God when they end up with less than favorable results from their prayers. Here are some of the excuses you may have heard when prayers are not answered: "It's not my time."; "It's not God's will."; "God gets the glory from my sickness."; " I need to fast a little while longer."

While all of these statements may be truly stated, they are not true. I know that sounds confusing, but stick with me, you will have a much better understanding soon.

Spiritual Laws

God has set forth spiritual laws in His Word regarding prayer. And unless the Word is rightly divided, many believers will experience times when their prayers will not be answered.

Let me ask a question.

If you bought a board game, no doubt a set of game rules would be included. To gain any kind of enjoyment from the game you would have to learn the rules. Even when you know the rules, there is a certain amount of skill required before you actually master the game.

Now, suppose you tried to use the rules of chess while playing Monopoly. The results would be rather disastrous, don't you think? Well, this is what is happening in the prayer lives of a number of believers. They have been trying to get results in prayer, but they have been using the wrong rules! Again I say, the reason prayers are not answered is that people do not pray according to God's Word.

There are several kinds of prayer mentioned in the Bible. Among those are the prayer of commitment, prayer of consecration, prayer of agreement, prayer of petition, and the prayer of worship. The subject of this book centers on the prayer of petition-the form of prayer used when asking God for something.

And all things, whatsoever ye shall ask in prayer, believing, ye shall receive. (Matthew 21:21)

Most people do not understand the principles of petition praying, and just how important a role the words they speak are. Instead of praying what the Word of God says about a certain situation, they tend to pray some unbelieving, faithless prayer like "If it be Thy will."

When God specifically addresses a certain subject and reveals His will in the matter, praying a prayer like this is faithless. Actually, it cancels out any faith that would have been attached to the prayer. The only time you should say those words is when you are praying the prayer of consecration.

Jesus prayed the prayer of consecration in the Garden of Gethsemane in order rededicate and submit his desires, steps, and thoughts to the Father.

"Saying, Father, if thou be willing, remove this cup from me: nevertheless not my will, but thine, be done (Luke 22:42)."

Whenever you consecrate yourself to God and submit your ways to Him so that He can order your steps, you should pray, "If it be Thy will." But if you are in need of something from God, that's not the prayer to pray. We already have God's Word concerning all of our needs. His Word is His Will. And His Word promises us that our needs can be met by asking in faith.

God is love and God is faithful to His people and His Word. There are times, however, when we tend to rely on our five physical senses to decide whether He is really "out there" and if He is hearing and answering our prayers of petition. Once we pray our prayers, all too often it's easy to look around for physical evidence and then believe for what we prayed.

When we do that, it's like trying to see with our ears or hear with our noses. We must determine even before we pray that any physical evidence contrary to what we pray will not sway us into doubt and unbelief. We need to realize that the evidence, or the Word upon which our faith rests is far more reliable than what we can see.

Regardless of physical evidence, the Word is perfect! It is the only thing that is guaranteed to "not come back void" or empty when properly applied.

Want to get good results when you pray? Every time you pray?

Pray the Word.

Listed below are some practical guidelines that guarantee you a successful prayer life.

1. **Commit your ways to God.** *"Commit thy way unto the Lord; trust also in him; and he shall bring it to pass" (Psalms 37:5).*

Make a quality decision to make God the Lord of everything in your life. If you are not a born-again Christian, or you have been wavering in your walk and need to rededicate your life, now is the time. God's promises do not apply to those walking in disobedience.

Don't hold onto those small things that you think you can handle on your own. It's the small foxes that spoil the vine. Cast ALL your cares upon the Lord. Take time to write all your cares and worries down. Then ball up the paper and throw it in the trash. Tell God according to His Word you cast all your cares on Him. Then stay out of the trash can!

This one step will eliminate the need to pray for peace, contentment, and stress release. Your deliverance will be experienced simply through obedience to the Word.

2. **Be specific about what you want from God.**
"But let him ask in faith, nothing wavering. For he that wavereth is like a wave of the sea driven with the wind and tossed. For let not that man think that

he shall receive any thing of the Lord. A double minded man is unstable in all his ways" (James 1:6-8).

This scripture teaches us that unless we make up our mind about our needs, and be specific, we cannot expect to have our requests met. General prayers like "Bless me, Lord," are a waste of time. You may as well go fishing.

If you had money in the bank, but went to the bank and only stood in the lobby rather than approach a cashier to make a withdrawal, it would be like you never had an account. The money is there, but you haven't put forth any effort to withdraw any of it.

What good does it do you?

The same applies to petition prayer.

Decide what you want, then be committed enough to it to continue believing until you have it.

3. **Find scripture to support what you are asking for, and then meditate on it**. *"If ye abide in me, and my words abide in you, ye shall ask what ye will, and it shall be done unto you" (John 15:7).*

The Bible contains over 7,000 promises, including promises of wealth, health, wisdom, and success. Finding the specific promises that apply to your situation may take some time, but it will be well worth the effort. As the seed of Abraham and a joint-heir with Jesus Christ, we have a bountiful inheritance that was left to us in His last WILL and (NEW) Testament.

Once you know you have been given or awarded something you simply have to lay your claim on it. Don't ask God for something, and cap it off with foolish words like "If it's Your will."

If a loved one passed and left you $1 million dollars you wouldn't go to his grave and ask "Is it your will that I have this million dollars?" You would march down to that lawyer's office, sign the necessary papers and ask for what YOU KNOW is already yours according to the last will and testament. You wouldn't be expecting more, or less. You know what the will said, and that's what you expect to receive.

4. Make your request known by asking in faith.
"Ask and it shall be given you: seek, and ye shall find; knock and the door shall be opened unto you" (Matthew 7:7).

"Therefore I say unto you, what things soever you desire, when you pray, believe that you receive them, and ye shall have them" (Mark 11:24). This step is important because if we don't actually get around to doing the asking we won't receive the answer. It's like looking in catalog and circling all the items you want to order but never getting around to ordering them. The key to praying the prayer of faith is you have to believe you have the answer WHEN you pray.

Start your confession of faith before you see the manifestation of your prayers answered. Hold fast to your confession by acting as though it were already done. To be afraid to confess or act before you have it is to doubt God's Word. You must also make sure you pray in Jesus' Name.

5. Rebuke doubt, fear and worry. *"Finally my brethren, whatsoever things are true, whatsoever things are honest, whatsoever things are just, whatsoever things are pure, whatsoever things are* *lovely, whatsoever things are of good report; if there be any virtue, and if there be any praise, think on these things" (Phil. 4:8).*

Faith to God is what fear is to Satan. It's the connection point. You are going to have to refuse to allow doubt and fear to enter your consciousness. Satan will whisper to you that your answers are not coming. But you have to take those whispers of doubt captive. Don't argue with the devil. Simply take the same position Jesus took when Satan tempted Him in the wilderness, and tell him "It is written!" Then begin to speak out loud whatever promise it is that you are standing on for your particular petition.

You have the right and power to demolish every argument that comes against the knowledge of God's Word. So control your mind with the Word and dwell on the answer instead of the problem. See yourself with the answer before it manifests. If you can't conceive it, then you won't have it.

6. **Testify, glorify and exude joy**. *"Be careful for nothing; but in every thing by prayer and supplication with thanksgiving let your requests be known unto God" (Phil.4:6).*

You must begin to testify of what you believe as if it has already happened. Testify of the Word. Add your testimony to what you have received by the Blood— your redemption. You have a right to all that Jesus did. Give God glory and praise continually.

The more you testify of God's goodness and blessings the sooner your manifestation will "catch up" to your confession. In Mark 11:23, we read that we will have what we SAY. So make sure you are saying only what the Word says about your situation and not what your circumstances say.

Happiness runs and hides whenever something unpleasant arises. But joy comes from complete reliance on the fact that God is faithful to produce everything He promised us in His Word. God's Word is His will. When we exercise our faith, His will is exercised! Faith It —'til You Make-It!!

7. **Give the answer to someone else.** *"Be not deceived; God is not mocked: for whatsoever a man soweth, that shall he also reap"(Gal. 6:7).*

Get on the giving end. If you need healing, then give the message of healing to someone else. If you need money, give money. If you want someone to cancel your debt then cancel the debt someone owes you. It is God's law that you will reap what you sow.

The way you measure out something is the way something will be measured back to you. By lifting someone else's burden, you build a foundation to harvest your own deliverance.

8. **Eliminate the "uns" in your life.**
There are a couple of things that hinder your prayers and keep them from being answered. I call them the "uns." You need to avoid them.

One of them is "unconfessed sin."

"If we confess our sins, he is faithful and just to forgive us our sins, and cleanse us from all unrighteousness. (1 John 1:9)

The other is "unforgiveness."

"And when ye stand praying, forgive, if ye have

ought against any: that your Father also which is in heaven may forgive you your trespasses. But if ye do not forgive, neither will your father which is heaven forgive your trespasses " (Mark 11:25-26).

Don't trip out when your prayers are not heard. If you are walking in sin and unforgiveness, then you should know your prayers are not going to be heard, let alone answered. Be honest with yourself. You may be able to fool man, but there is no fooling God. Confess the sin, receive God's forgiveness and get on with life. Face the music and make the necessary changes so every prayer in your life will be heard, and answered!

Wrap Up!

Begin to search the scriptures daily. Proverbs, Psalms and the New Testament books of Matthew, Mark, Luke, and John are rich with promises and are a good place to start your daily meditation and confession.

Watch out for Satan's ploy to steal the Word from your heart as quickly as you receive it. That's his goal. But you'll have to discipline yourself, and your flesh to stay on the Word and get it down inside you.

It will be well worth it in the long run.

In addition, don't be surprised if once you commit to spending quality time in the Word all kinds of distractions arise to keep you from the Word. The phone may ring, or someone may knock at the door. You may even find yourself getting sleepy. But don't fall for it. It's just a trick of the enemy. The Bible says he comes to steal the Word.

Don't let him. Say, like Jesus said, "Satan, get thee behind me!" Then add: "NOW!"

The following is a list of God's promises in specific

areas to get you started. As you pray each prayer, be sure and insert your name, or the name of the person you are praying for, so that the prayer becomes more personal. (Ex. The Lord is (your name) my Shepherd. (Your name) shall not want.

Finances

Psalms 23:1

"The LORD is my shepherd; I shall not want."

Malachi 3:10-12

"Bring ye all the tithes into the storehouse, that there may be meat in mine house, and prove me now herewith, saith the LORD of hosts, if I will not open you the windows of heaven, and pour you out a blessing, that there shall not be room enough to receive it. And I will rebuke the devourer for your sakes, and he shall not destroy the fruits of your ground; neither shall your vine cast her fruit before the time in the field, saith the LORD of hosts. And all nations shall call you blessed: for ye shall be a delightsome land, saith the LORD of hosts."

3 John 1:2

"Beloved, I wish above all things that thou mayest prosper and be in health, even as thy soul prospereth."

Joshua 1:8

"This book of the law shall not depart out of thy mouth; but thou shalt meditate therein day and night, that thou mayest observe to do according to all that is written therein: for then thou shalt make thy way prosperous, and then thou shalt have good success."

Philippians 4:19

"But my God shall supply all your need according to his riches in glory by Christ Jesus."

2 Corinthians 9:6-8

"But this I say, He which soweth sparingly shall reap also sparingly; and he which soweth bountifully shall reap also bountifully. Every man according as he purposeth in his heart, so let him give; not grudgingly, or of necessity: for God loveth a cheerful giver. And God is able to make all grace abound toward you; that ye, always having all sufficiency in all things, may abound to every good work."

Psalms 37:25

"I have been young, and now am old; yet have I not seen the righteous forsaken, nor his seed begging bread."

Psalms 34:10

"The young lions do lack, and suffer hunger: but they that seek the LORD shall not want any good thing."

Deuteronomy 28:2-8

"And all these blessings shall come on thee, and overtake thee, if thou shalt hearken unto the voice of the LORD thy God. Blessed shalt thou be in the city, and blessed shalt thou be in the field. Blessed shall be the fruit of thy body, and the fruit of thy ground, and the fruit of thy cattle, the increase of thy kine, and the flocks of thy sheep. Blessed shall be thy basket and thy store. Blessed shalt thou be when thou comest in, and blessed shalt thou be when thou goest out. The LORD shall cause thine enemies that rise up against thee to be smitten before thy face: they shall come out against thee one way, and flee before thee seven ways. The LORD shall command the blessing upon thee in thy storehouses, and in all that thou settest thine hand unto; and he shall bless thee in the land which the LORD thy God giveth thee."

Deuteronomy 28:11-13
"And the LORD shall make thee plenteous in goods, in the fruit of thy body, and in the fruit of thy cattle, and in the fruit of thy ground, in the land which the LORD sware unto thy fathers to give thee. The LORD shall open unto thee his good treasure, the heaven to give the rain unto thy land in his season, and to bless all the work of thine hand: and thou shalt lend unto many nations, and thou shalt not borrow. And the LORD shall make thee the head, and not the tail; and thou shalt be above only, and thou shalt not be beneath; if that thou hearken unto the commandments of the LORD thy God, which I command thee this day, to observe and to do them."

Luke 6:38
"Give, and it shall be given unto you; good measure, pressed down, and shaken together, and running over, shall men give into your bosom. For with the same measure that ye mete withal it shall be measured to you again. "

1 Corinthians 16:2
"Upon the first day of the week let every one of you lay by him in store, as God hath prospered him, that there be no gatherings when I come."

Matthew 19:29

"And every one that hath forsaken houses, or brethren, or sisters, or father, or mother, or wife, or children, or lands, for my name's sake, shall receive an hundredfold, and shall inherit everlasting life."

Ecclesiastes 2:26

"For God giveth to a man that is good in his sight wisdom, and knowledge, and joy: but to the sinner he giveth travail, to gather and to heap up, that he may give to him that is good before God. This also is vanity and vexation of spirit."

Deuteronomy 8:18

"But thou shalt remember the LORD thy God: for it is he that giveth thee power to get wealth, that he may establish his covenant which he sware unto thy fathers, as it is this day.

Matthew 6:31-33

"Therefore take no thought, saying, What shall we eat? or, What shall we drink? or, Wherewithal shall we be clothed? (For after all these things do the Gentiles seek:) for your heavenly Father knoweth that ye have need of all these things. But seek ye first the kingdom of God, and his righteousness; and all these things shall be added unto you."

Healing

Matthew 9:35

"And Jesus went about all the cities and villages, teaching in their synagogues, and preaching the gospel of the kingdom, and healing every sickness and every disease among the people."

Proverbs 4:20-22

"My son, attend to my words; incline thine ear unto my sayings. Let them not depart from thine eyes; keep them in the midst of thine heart. For they are life unto those that find them, and health to all their flesh."

Psalms 107:20

"He sent his word, and healed them, and delivered them from their destructions."

Matthew 8:8

"The centurion answered and said, Lord, I am not worthy that thou shouldest come under my roof: but speak the word only, and my servant shall be healed."

3 John 2:1

"Beloved, I wish above all things that thou mayest prosper and be in health, even as thy soul prospereth."

James 5:14-15

"Is any sick among you? let him call for the elders of the church; and let them pray over him, anointing him with oil in the name of the Lord: And the prayer of faith shall save the sick, and the Lord shall raise him up; and if he have committed sins, they shall be forgiven him.'

Mark 16:17-18

"And these signs shall follow them that believe; In my name shall they cast out devils; they shall speak with new tongues; They shall take up serpents; and if they drink any deadly thing, it shall not hurt them; they shall lay hands on the sick, and they shall recover."

Jeremiah 17:14
"Heal me, O LORD, and I shall be healed; save me, and I shall be saved: for thou art my praise."

Jeremiah 30:17
"For I will restore health unto thee, and I will heal thee of thy wounds, saith the LORD; because they called thee an Outcast, saying, This is Zion, whom no man seeketh after."

Exodus 15:26
"And said, If thou wilt diligently hearken to the voice of the LORD thy God, and wilt do that which is right in his sight, and wilt give ear to his commandments, and keep all his statutes, I will put none of these diseases upon thee, which I have brought upon the Egyptians: for I am the LORD that healeth thee."

Luke 6:19
"And the whole multitude sought to touch him: for there went virtue out of him, and healed them all."

Hebrews 13:8
"Jesus Christ the same yesterday, and to day, and for ever."

1 Peter 2:24
"Who his own self bare our sins in his own body on the tree, that we, being dead to sins, should live unto righteousness: by whose stripes ye were healed."

Psalms 103:3

"Who forgiveth all thine iniquities; who healeth all thy diseases."

Isaiah 53:5

"But he was wounded for our transgressions, he was bruised for our iniquities: the chastisement of our peace was upon him; and with his stripes we are healed."

Marital Harmony
1 Peter 3:1-11

"Likewise, ye wives, be in subjection to your own husbands; that, if any obey not the word, they also may without the word be won by the conversation of the wives; While they behold your chaste conversation coupled with fear. Whose adorning let it not be that outward adorning of plaiting the hair, and of wearing of gold, or of putting on of apparel; But let it be the hidden man of the heart, in that which is not corruptible, even the ornament of a meek and quiet spirit, which is in the sight of God of great price. For after this manner in the old time the holy women also, who trusted in God, adorned themselves, being in subjection unto their own husbands: Even as Sara obeyed Abraham, calling him lord: whose daughters ye are, as long as ye do well, and are not afraid with any amazement. Likewise, ye husbands, dwell with them according to knowledge, giving honour unto the wife, as unto the weaker vessel, and as being heirs together of the grace of life; that your prayers be not hindered. Finally, be ye all of one mind, having compassion one of another, love as brethren, be pitiful, be courteous: Not rendering evil for evil, or railing for railing: but contrariwise blessing; knowing that ye are thereunto called, that ye should inherit a blessing. For he that will love life, and see good days, let him refrain his tongue from evil, and his lips that they speak no guile: Let him eschew evil, and do good; let him seek peace, and ensue it."

Joshua 24:15
"And if it seem evil unto you to serve the LORD, choose you this day whom ye will serve; whether the gods which your fathers served that were on the other side of the flood, or the gods of the Amorites, in whose land ye dwell: but as for me and my house, we will serve the LORD."

Ephesians 4:31-32
"Let all bitterness, and wrath, and anger, and clamour, and evil speaking, be put away from you, with all malice: And be ye kind one to another, tenderhearted, forgiving one another, even as God for Christ's sake hath forgiven you."

Genesis 2:18
"And the LORD God said, It is not good that the man should be alone; I will make him an help meet for him."

Genesis 2:24
"Therefore shall a man leave his father and his mother, and shall cleave unto his wife: and they shall be one flesh."

Ephesians 5:21-33
"Submitting yourselves one to another in the fear of God. Wives, submit yourselves unto your own husbands, as unto the Lord. For the husband is the head

of the wife, even as Christ is the head of the church: and he is the saviour of the body. Therefore as the church is subject unto Christ, so let the wives be to their own husbands in every thing. Husbands, love your wives, even as Christ also loved the church, and gave himself for it; That he might sanctify and cleanse it with the washing of water by the word, That he might present it to himself a glorious church, not having spot, or wrinkle, or any such thing; but that it should be holy and without blemish. So ought men to love their wives as their own bodies. He that loveth his wife loveth himself. For no man ever yet hated his own flesh; but nourisheth and cherisheth it, even as the Lord the church: For we are members of his body, of his flesh, and of his bones. For this cause shall a man leave his father and mother, and shall be joined unto his wife, and they two shall be one flesh. This is a great mystery: but I speak concerning Christ and the church. Nevertheless let every one of you in particular so love his wife even as himself; and the wife see that she reverence her husband."

Romans 13:10
"Love worketh no ill to his neighbour: therefore love is the fulfilling of the law."

Psalms 101:2
"I will behave myself wisely in a perfect way. O when wilt thou come unto me? I will walk within my house with a perfect heart."

Proverbs 3:5-6
"Trust in the LORD with all thine heart; and lean not unto thine own understanding. In all thy ways

acknowledge him, and he shall direct thy paths."

Proverbs 10:12

"Hatred stirreth up strifes: but love covereth all sins."

1 Peter 1:22

"Seeing ye have purified your souls in obeying the truth through the Spirit unto unfeigned love of the brethren, see that ye love one another with a pure heart fervently."

Loneliness

Hebrews 13:5

"Let your conversation be without covetousness; and be content with such things as ye have: for he hath said, I will never leave thee, nor forsake thee."

Psalms 147:3

"He healeth the broken in heart, and bindeth up their wounds."

Matthew 28:20

"Teaching them to observe all things whatsoever I have commanded you: and, lo, I am with you always, even unto the end of the world. Amen."

1 Samuel 12:22

"For the LORD will not forsake his people for his great name's sake: because it hath pleased the LORD to make you his people."

Isaiah 41:10

"Fear thou not; for I am with thee: be not dismayed; for I am thy God: I will strengthen thee; yea, I will help thee; yea, I will uphold thee with the right hand of my righteousness."

Isaiah 54:10

"For the mountains shall depart, and the hills be removed; but my kindness shall not depart from thee, neither shall the covenant of my peace be removed, saith the LORD that hath mercy on thee."

Psalms 27:10

"When my father and my mother forsake me, then the LORD will take me up."

Psalms 46:1

"God is our refuge and strength, a very present help in trouble."

John 14:1

"Let not your heart be troubled: ye believe in God, believe also in me."

Deuteronomy 4:31

"(For the LORD thy God is a merciful God;) he will not forsake thee, neither destroy thee, nor forget the covenant of thy fathers which he sware unto them."

Deuteronomy 31:6

"Be strong and of a good courage, fear not, nor be afraid of them: for the LORD thy God, he it is that doth go with thee; he will not fail thee, nor forsake thee."

Deuteronomy 33:27

"The eternal God is thy refuge, and underneath are the everlasting arms: and he shall thrust out the enemy from before thee; and shall say, Destroy them."

Romans 8:35-39

"Who shall separate us from the love of Christ? shall tribulation, or distress, or persecution, or famine, or nakedness, or peril, or sword? As it is written, For thy sake we are killed all the day long; we are accounted as sheep for the slaughter. Nay, in all these things we are more than conquerors through him that loved us. For I am persuaded, that neither death, nor life, nor angels, nor principalities, nor powers, nor things present, nor things to come, Nor height, nor depth, nor any other creature, shall be able to separate us from the love of God, which is in Christ Jesus our Lord."

1 Peter 5:7

"Casting all your care upon him; for he careth for you."

Patience

Psalms 27:14

"Wait on the LORD: be of good courage, and he shall strengthen thine heart: wait, I say, on the LORD."

Psalms 33:20

"Our soul waiteth for the LORD: he is our help and our shield."

Psalms 62:5

"My soul, wait thou only upon God; for my expectation is from him."

Psalms 130:5

"I wait for the LORD, my soul doth wait, and in his word do I hope."

Psalms 145:15-16

"The eyes of all wait upon thee; and thou givest them their meat in due season. Thou openest thine hand, and satisfiest the desire of every living thing."

Isaiah 25:9

"And it shall be said in that day, Lo, this is our God; we have waited for him, and he will save us: this is the LORD; we have waited for him, we will be glad and rejoice in his salvation."

Isaiah 40:31

"But they that wait upon the LORD shall renew their strength; they shall mount up with wings as eagles; they shall run, and not be weary; and they shall walk, and not faint."

Habakkuk 2:3

"For the vision is yet for an appointed time, but at the end it shall speak, and not lie: though it tarry, wait for it; because it will surely come, it will not tarry."

Hebrews 3:14

"For we are made partakers of Christ, if we hold the beginning of our confidence stedfast unto the end."

Hebrews 10:23

"Let us hold fast the profession of our faith without wavering; (for he is faithful that promised;)"

Contentment

Psalms 34:10

"The young lions do lack, and suffer hunger: but they that seek the LORD shall not want any good thing."

Isaiah 44:3

"For I will pour water upon him that is thirsty, and floods upon the dry ground: I will pour my spirit upon thy seed, and my blessing upon thine offspring:

Psalms 37:3

"Trust in the LORD, and do good; so shalt thou dwell in the land, and verily thou shalt be fed."

Philippians 4:12, 13

"I know both how to be abased, and I know how to abound: every where and
in all things I am instructed both to be full and to be hungry, both to abound and to suffer need. I can do all things through Christ which strengtheneth me."

Psalms 63:1-5

"O God, thou art my God; early will I seek thee: my soul thirsteth for thee, my flesh longeth for thee in a dry and thirsty land, where no water is; To see thy power and thy glory, so as I have seen thee in the sanctuary. Because thy lovingkindness is better than life, my lips shall praise thee. Thus will I bless thee while I live: I will lift up my hands in thy name. My soul shall be satisfied as with marrow and fatness; and my mouth shall praise thee with joyful lips."

Proverbs 12:14
"A man shall be satisfied with good by the fruit of his mouth: and the recompence of a man's hands shall be rendered unto him."

Jeremiah 31:14
"...and my people shall be satisfied with my goodness, saith the LORD."

Joel 2:26
"And ye shall eat in plenty, and be satisfied, and praise the name of the LORD your God, that hath dealt wondrously with you: and my people shall never be ashamed."

Psalms 103:1-5
"Bless the LORD, O my soul: and all that is within me, bless his holy name. Bless the LORD, O my soul, and forget not all his benefits: Who forgiveth all thine iniquities; who healeth all thy diseases; Who redeemeth thy life from destruction; who crowneth thee with lovingkindness and tender mercies; Who satisfieth thy mouth with good things; so that thy youth is renewed like the eagle's."

Psalms 107:9
"For he satisfieth the longing soul, and filleth the hungry soul with goodness."

Isaiah 12:2, 3

"Behold, God is my salvation; I will trust, and not be afraid: for the LORD JEHOVAH is my strength and my song; he also is become my salvation. Therefore with joy shall ye draw water out of the wells of salvation."

2 Corinthians 9:8

"And God is able to make all grace abound toward you; that ye, always having all sufficiency in all things, may abound to every good work."

Isaiah 55:1

"Ho, every one that thirsteth, come ye to the waters, and he that hath no money; come ye, buy, and eat; yea, come, buy wine and milk without money and without price."

Matthew 5:6

"Blessed are they which do hunger and thirst after righteousness: for they shall be filled."

Temptation/Discouragement

Isaiah 51:11

"Therefore the redeemed of the LORD shall return, and come with singing unto Zion; and everlasting joy shall be upon their head: they shall obtain gladness and joy; and sorrow and mourning shall flee away."

1 Peter 1:6-9

"Wherein ye greatly rejoice, though now for a season, if need be, ye are in heaviness through manifold temptations: That the trial of your faith, being much more precious than of gold that perisheth, though it be tried with fire, might be found unto praise and honour and glory at the appearing of Jesus Christ: Whom having not seen, ye love; in whom, though now ye see him not, yet believing, ye rejoice with joy unspeakable and full of glory: Receiving the end of your faith, even the salvation of your souls."

Philippians 4:6-8
"Be careful for nothing; but in every thing by prayer and supplication with thanksgiving let your requests be made known unto God. And the peace of God, which passeth all understanding, shall keep your hearts and minds through Christ Jesus. Finally, brethren, whatsoever things are true, whatsoever things are honest, whatsoever things are just, whatsoever things are pure, whatsoever things are lovely, whatsoever things are of good report; if there be any virtue, and if there be any praise, think on these things."

Psalms 138:7
"Though I walk in the midst of trouble, thou wilt revive me: thou shalt stretch forth thine hand against the wrath of mine enemies, and thy right hand shall save me."

John 14:1
"Let not your heart be troubled: ye believe in God, believe also in me."

John 14:27
"Peace I leave with you, my peace I give unto you: not as the world giveth, give I unto you. Let not your heart be troubled, neither let it be afraid."

2 Corinthians 4:8-9

"We are troubled on every side, yet not distressed; we are perplexed, but not in despair; Persecuted, but not forsaken; cast down, but not destroyed;"

Hebrews 10:35-36

"Cast not away therefore your confidence, which hath great recompence of reward. For ye have need of patience, that, after ye have done the will of God, ye might receive the promise."

Philippians 1:6

"Being confident of this very thing, that he which hath begun a good work in you will perform it until the day of Jesus Christ:"

Galatians 6:9

"And let us not be weary in well doing: for in due season we shall reap, if we faint not."

Psalms 31:24

"Be of good courage, and he shall strengthen your heart, all ye that hope in the LORD."

Psalms 27:1-14

"The LORD is my light and my salvation; whom shall I fear? the LORD is the strength of my life; of whom shall I be afraid? When the wicked, even mine enemies and my foes, came upon me to eat up my flesh, they stumbled and fell. Though an host should encamp against me, my heart shall not fear: though war should rise against me, in this will I be confident. One thing have I desired of the LORD, that will I seek after; that I may dwell in the house of the LORD all the days of my life, to behold the beauty of the LORD, and to enquire in his temple. For in the time of trouble he shall hide me in his pavilion: in the secret of his tabernacle shall he hide me; he shall set me up upon a rock. And now shall mine head be lifted up above mine enemies round about me: therefore will I offer in his tabernacle sacrifices of joy; I will sing, yea, I will sing praises unto the LORD. Hear, O LORD, when I cry with my voice: have mercy also upon me, and answer me. When thou saidst, Seek ye my face; my heart said unto thee, Thy face, LORD, will I seek. Hide not thy face far from me; put not thy servant away in anger: thou hast been my help; leave me not, neither forsake me, O God of my salvation. When my father and my mother forsake me, then the LORD will take me up. Teach me thy way, O LORD, and lead me in a plain path, because of mine enemies. Deliver me not over unto the will of mine enemies: for false witnesses are risen up against me, and such as breathe out cruelty. I had fainted, unless I had believed to see the goodness of the LORD in the land of the living."

1 Corinthians 10:12, 13

"Wherefore let him that thinketh he standeth take heed lest he fall...There hath no temptation taken you but such as is common to man: but God is faithful, who will not suffer you to be tempted above that ye are able; but will with the temptation also make a way to escape, that ye may be able to bear it."

Hebrews 4:14-16

"Seeing then that we have a great high priest, that is passed into the heavens, Jesus the Son of God, let us hold fast our profession. For we have not an high priest which cannot be touched with the feeling of our infirmities; but was in all points tempted like as we are, yet without sin. Let us therefore come boldly unto the throne of grace, that we may obtain mercy, and find grace to help in time of need."

Hebrews 2:18
"For in that he himself hath suffered being tempted, he is able to succour them that are tempted."

2 Peter 2:9
"The Lord knoweth how to deliver the godly out of temptations..."

Romans 6:14
"For sin shall not have dominion over you: for ye are not under the law, but under grace."

Psalms 119:11
"Thy word have I hid in mine heart, that I might not sin against thee."

James 1:13, 14
"Let no man say when he is tempted, I am tempted of God: for God cannot be tempted with evil, neither tempteth he any man: But every man is tempted, when he is drawn away of his own lust, and enticed."

Proverbs 28:13
"He that covereth his sins shall not prosper: but whoso confesseth and forsaketh them shall have mercy."

1 John 1:9

"If we confess our sins, he is faithful and just to forgive us our sins, and to cleanse us from all unrighteousness."

1 Peter 5:8, 9

"Be sober, be vigilant; because your adversary the devil, as a roaring lion, walketh about, seeking whom he may devour: Whom resist stedfast in the faith, knowing that the same afflictions are accomplished in your brethren that are in the world."

Ephesians 6:10, 11, 16

"Finally, my brethren, be strong in the Lord, and in the power of his might. Put on the whole armour of God, that ye may be able to stand against the wiles of the devil...Above all, taking the shield of faith, wherewith ye shall be able to quench all the fiery darts of the wicked."

James 4:7

"Submit yourselves therefore to God. Resist the devil, and he will flee from you."

1 John 4:4

"Ye are of God, little children, and have overcome them: because greater is he that is in you, than he that is in the world."

James 1:2, 3, 12

"My brethren, count it all joy when ye fall into divers temptations; Knowing this, that the trying of your faith worketh patience...Blessed is the man that endureth temptation: for when he is tried, he shall receive the crown of life, which the Lord hath promised to them that love him."

1 Peter 1:6, 7

"Wherein ye greatly rejoice, though now for a season, if need be, ye are in heaviness through manifold temptations: That the trial of your faith, being much more precious than of gold that perisheth, though it be tried with fire, might be found unto praise and honour and glory at the appearing of Jesus Christ."

Confidence/Determination

Philippians 4:13

"I can do all things through Christ which strengtheneth me."

Hebrews 13:6

"So that we may boldly say, The Lord is my helper, and I will not fear what man shall do unto me."

Hebrews 10:35, 36

"Cast not away therefore your confidence, which hath great recompence of reward. For ye have need of patience, that, after ye have done the will of God, ye might receive the promise."

Philippians 1:6

"Being confident of this very thing, that he which hath begun a good work in you will perform it until the day of Jesus Christ."

Habakkuk 3:19

"The LORD God is my strength, and he will make

my feet like hinds' feet, and he will make me to walk upon mine high places. To the chief singer on my stringed instruments."

Romans 8:37

"Nay, in all these things we are more than conquerors through him that loved us."

1 John 5:14, 15

"And this is the confidence that we have in him, that, if we ask any thing according to his will, he heareth us: And if we know that he hear us, whatsoever we ask, we know that we have the petitions that we desired of him."

John 14:12

"Verily, verily, I say unto you, He that believeth on me, the works that I do shall he do also; and greater works than these shall he do; because I go unto my Father."

Zechariah 4:6

"Then he answered and spake unto me, saying, This is the word of the LORD unto Zerubbabel, saying, Not by might, nor by power, but by my spirit, saith the LORD of hosts."

Isaiah 43:2

"When thou passest through the waters, I will be with thee; and through the rivers, they shall not overflow thee: when thou walkest through the fire, thou shalt not be burned; neither shall the flame kindle upon thee."

Proverbs 3:26

"For the LORD shall be thy confidence, and shall keep thy foot from being taken."

2 Corinthians 7:16

"I rejoice therefore that I have confidence in you in all things."

Ephesians 3:12

"In whom we have boldness and access with confidence by the faith of him."

1 John 3:21

"Beloved, if our heart condemn us not, then have we confidence toward God."

Isaiah 40:31

"But they that wait upon the LORD shall renew their strength; they shall mount up with wings as eagles; they shall run, and not be weary; and they shall walk, and not faint."

Fear/Worry/Depression

2 Timothy 1:7

"For God hath not given us the spirit of fear; but of power, and of love, and of a sound mind."

Romans 8:15

"For ye have not received the spirit of bondage again to fear; but ye have received the Spirit of adoption, whereby we cry, Abba, Father."

1 John 4:18

"There is no fear in love; but perfect love casteth out

fear: because fear hath torment. He that feareth is not made perfect in love."

Psalms 91:1
"He that dwelleth in the secret place of the most High shall abide under the shadow of the Almighty."

Psalms 91:4-7
"He shall cover thee with his feathers, and under his wings shalt thou trust: his truth shall be thy shield and buckler. Thou shalt not be afraid for the terror by night; nor for the arrow that flieth by day; Nor for the pestilence that walketh in darkness; nor for the destruction that wasteth at noonday. A thousand shall fall at thy side, and ten thousand at thy right hand; but it shall not come nigh thee."

Psalms 91:10, 11
"There shall no evil befall thee, neither shall any plague come nigh thy dwelling. For he shall give his angels charge over thee, to keep thee in all thy ways."

Proverbs 3:25, 26
"Be not afraid of sudden fear, neither of the desolation of the wicked, when it cometh. For the LORD shall be thy confidence, and shall keep thy foot from being taken."

Isaiah 54:14
"In righteousness shalt thou be established: thou shalt be far from oppression; for thou shalt not fear: and from terror; for it shall not come near thee."

Psalms 56:11

"In God have I put my trust: I will not be afraid what man can do unto me."

Psalms 23:4, 5

"Yea, though I walk through the valley of the shadow of death, I will fear no evil: for thou art with me; thy rod and thy staff they comfort me. Thou preparest a table before me in the presence of mine enemies: thou anointest my head with oil; my cup runneth over."

Romans 8:29, 31, 35-39

"For whom he did foreknow, he also did predestinate to be conformed to the image of his Son, that he might be the firstborn among many brethren...What shall we then say to these things? If God be for us, who can be against us?

"Who shall separate us from the love of Christ? shall tribulation, or distress, or persecution, or famine, or nakedness, or peril, or sword? As it is written, For thy sake we are killed all the day long; we are accounted as sheep for the slaughter. Nay, in all these things we are more than conquerors through him that loved us. For I am persuaded, that neither death, nor life, nor angels, nor principalities, nor powers, nor things present, nor things to come, Nor height, nor depth, nor any other creature, shall be able to separate us from the love of God, which is in Christ Jesus our Lord."

Psalms 31:24

"Be of good courage, and he shall strengthen your heart, all ye that hope in the LORD."

John 14:27

"Peace I leave with you, my peace I give unto you: not as the world giveth, give I unto you. Let not your heart be troubled, neither let it be afraid."

Psalms 27:1, 3

"The LORD is my light and my salvation; whom shall I fear? the LORD is the strength of my life; of whom shall I be afraid...Though an host should encamp against me, my heart shall not fear: though war should rise against me, in this will I be confident."

1 Peter 5:7

"Casting all your care upon him; for he careth for you.

John 14:15

"Let not your heart be troubled: ye believe in God, believe also in me."

Philippians 4:6, 7

"Be careful for nothing; but in every thing by prayer and supplication with thanksgiving let your requests be made known unto God. And the peace of God, which passeth all understanding, shall keep your hearts and minds through Christ Jesus."

Colossians 3:15

"And let the peace of God rule in your hearts, to the which also ye are
called in one body; and be ye thankful."

Isaiah 26:3

"Thou wilt keep him in perfect peace, whose mind is

stayed on thee: because he trusteth in thee."

Psalms 4:8
"I will both lay me down in peace, and sleep: for thou, LORD, only makest me dwell in safety."

Philippians 4:19
"But my God shall supply all your need according to his riches in glory by Christ Jesus."

Matthew 6:25-34
"Therefore I say unto you, Take no thought for your life, what ye shall eat, or what ye shall drink; nor yet for your body, what ye shall put on. Is not the life more than meat, and the body than raiment? Behold the fowls of the air: for they sow not, neither do they reap, nor gather into barns; yet your heavenly Father feedeth them. Are ye not much better than they? Which of you by taking thought can add one cubit unto his stature? And why take ye thought for raiment? Consider the lilies of the field, how they grow; they toil not, neither do they spin: And yet I say unto you, That even Solomon in all his glory was not arrayed like one of these.

"Wherefore, if God so clothe the grass of the field, which to day is, and tomorrow is cast into the oven, shall he not much more clothe you, O ye of little faith? Therefore take no thought, saying, What shall we eat? or, What shall we drink? or, Wherewithal shall we be clothed? (For after all these things do the Gentiles seek:) for your heavenly Father knoweth that ye have need of all these things. But seek ye first the kingdom of God, and his righteousness; and all these things shall be added unto you. Take therefore no thought for the morrow: for the morrow shall take thought for the things of itself. Sufficient unto the day is the evil thereof."

Romans 8:6
"For to be carnally minded is death; but to be spiritually minded is life and peace."

Proverbs 3:24
"When thou liest down, thou shalt not be afraid: yea, thou shalt lie down, and thy sleep shall be sweet."

Hebrews 4:3, 9

"For we which have believed do enter into rest, as he said, As I have sworn in my wrath, if they shall enter into my rest: although the works were finished from the foundation of the world...There remaineth therefore a rest to the people of God."

Psalms 119:165
"Great peace have they which love thy law: and nothing shall offend them."

Psalms 91:1, 2
"He that dwelleth in the secret place of the most High shall abide under the shadow of the Almighty. I will say of the LORD, He is my refuge and my fortress: my God; in him will I trust."

John 14:27
"Peace I leave with you, my peace I give unto you: not as the world giveth, give I unto you. Let not your heart be troubled, neither let it be afraid."

Psalms 30:5

"For his anger endureth but a moment; in his favour is life: weeping may endure for a night, but joy cometh in the morning."

Psalms 34:17

"The righteous cry, and the LORD heareth, and delivereth them out of all their troubles."

Psalms 147:3

"He healeth the broken in heart, and bindeth up their wounds."

Isaiah 40:31

"But they that wait upon the LORD shall renew their strength; they shall mount up with wings as eagles; they shall run, and not be weary; and they shall walk, and not faint."

Isaiah 41:10

"Fear thou not; for I am with thee: be not dismayed; for I am thy God: I will strengthen thee; yea, I will help thee; yea, I will uphold thee with the right hand of my righteousness."

Isaiah 43:2

"When thou passest through the waters, I will be with thee; and through the rivers, they shall not overflow thee: when thou walkest through the fire, thou shalt not be burned; neither shall the flame kindle upon thee."

Isaiah 61:3

"To appoint unto them that mourn in Zion, to give

unto them beauty for ashes, the oil of joy for mourning, the garment of praise for the spirit of heaviness; that they might be called trees of righteousness, the planting of the LORD, that he might be glorified."

1 Peter 4:12-13

"Beloved, think it not strange concerning the fiery trial which is to try you, as though some strange thing happened unto you: But rejoice, inasmuch as ye are partakers of Christ's sufferings; that, when his glory shall be revealed, ye may be glad also with exceeding joy."

Luke 18:1

"And he spake a parable unto them to this end, that men ought always to
pray, and not to faint."

2 Corinthians 1:3-4

"Blessed be God, even the Father of our Lord Jesus Christ, the Father of mercies, and the God of all comfort; Who comforteth us in all our tribulation, that we may be able to comfort them which are in any trouble, by the comfort wherewith we ourselves are comforted of God."

Romans 8:38-39

"For I am persuaded, that neither death, nor life, nor angels, nor principalities, nor powers, nor things present, nor things to come, Nor height, nor depth, nor any other creature, shall be able to separate us from the love of God, which is in Christ Jesus our Lord."

Philippians 4:18

"But I have all, and abound: I am full, having received of Epaphroditus
the things which were sent from you, an odour of a sweet smell, a
sacrifice acceptable, wellpleasing to God."

1 Peter 5:6-7

"Humble yourselves therefore under the mighty hand of God, that he may
exalt you in due time: Casting all your care upon him; for he careth for you."

www.Faith-It-Til-You-Make-It.com

A Prayer for Salvation and Baptism
of the Holy Ghost

Heavenly Father, I come to You in the Name of Jesus. Your Word says, "Whosoever shall call on the name of the Lord shall be saved" (Acts 2:21). I am calling on You now.

I ask Jesus to come into my heart and be Lord over my life according to Romans 10:9-10, which says *"If thou shalt confess with thy mouth the Lord Jesus, and shalt believe in thine heart that God hath raised him from the dead, thou shalt be saved."* I do that now. I believe in my heart that God raised Jesus from the dead, and I confess now that Jesus is Lord over my life. I am now reborn! I am a Christian—a child of Almighty God! I am saved! Father, You also said in Your Word, *"If ye then, being evil, know how to give good gifts unto your children: HOW MUCH MORE shall your heavenly Father give the Holy Spirit to them that ask him?" (Luke 11:13). I'm also asking You to fill me with the Holy Spirit. Holy Spirit, rise up within me as I praise God. I fully expect to speak with other tongues as You give me the utterance (Acts 2:4).*

Now, begin to praise God for filling you with the Holy Spirit. Speak those words and syllables you receive—not in your own language, but the language given to you by the Holy Spirit. You have to use your own voice. God will not force you to speak.

Now you are a Spirit-filled believer!

Continue with the blessing God has given you and pray in tongues every day. You'll never be the same! Find a good church that preaches the Word of God, and become a part of a church family who will love and care for you as you love and care for them. We need to be hooked up to each other. It increases our strength in God. It's God's plan for us. Write and let us know how you are doing in your new life as a believer.

Future Titles From Ben and Jewel Tankard

Get Over It!
Soulmate or Cellmate
Modeled in His Image

For Concert/Speaking Bookings and to order products, contact:

Ben Tankard Ministries
P.O. Box 11594
Murfreesboro, TN 37129
(615) 207-6685 phone
(615) 907-6729 fax
www.bentankardministries.com
bentankard@aol.com

Ben-Jamin' Publishing

Faith It—'til You Make It!
By Ben Tankard

Faith Nuggets *from an NBA hopeful who suffered a career ending injury, poverty, divorce, and the death of both parents only to rebound and use his faith to become a nationally recognized, best-selling gospel jazz recording artist !*

Expectation is the breeding ground for miracles!

Faith It—'til You Make It! reveals the pain behind Ben Tankard's passion and how despite his talents, he did not step into consistent increase, marital harmony, spiritual or material success until he put God first and began to walk by faith. **Chapters include**: ***From Test to Testimony;Faith It—'til You Make It!; How to Be a Rich Christian,*** and ***Every Prayer Answered.*** No matter where you are in life, ***Faith It—'til You Make It!*** will challenge, motivate, inspire and encourage you. The best is yet to come!

The Author: **Ben Tankard,** widely recognized as the "Godfather of Gospel Jazz," is the recipient of nine Stellar Awards and multiple Dove and Grammy nominations. He has recorded 13 top instrumental solo albums and collaborated on over 500 recordings in his 13-year career (including work with platinum artists **Fred Hammond, Kelly Price, Take-6 and Yolanda**

Adams). Ben's teaching ministry was jump-started by a prophetic word, and an anointing by **Dr. Creflo A. Dollar Jr.**

Ben and his wife, Jewel, pastor the fast-growing *Destiny Center* in Murfreesboro/Lebanon, Tenn. and are internationally recognized through record distribution, radio broadcast, and personal and TV appearances.

The Tankards reside in Murfreesboro, Tenn. with their children.

www.Faith-It-Til-You-Make-It.com

1.800.249.4427